THE

HIDDEN PLACES

of

Lancashire, Cheshire

& The Isle of Man

3rd Edition

Front Cover:
Lyme Hall, Cheshire
by Les Darlow

ACKNOWLEDGEMENTS

This book would not have been compiled without the dedicated help of the following:
Elaine, Hong - Administration. Les & Graham - Artists. Bob, Harvey, Jim, Dave -
Research. Alice, Jenny and Hattie - Editing. Chris - DTP.

Map origination by Paul and Simon at Legend DTP, Stockport, 061 419-9748

All have contributed to what we hope is an interesting, useful and enjoyable publication.

OTHER TITLES IN THIS SERIES

The Hidden Places of Devon and Cornwall
The Hidden Places of East Anglia
The Hidden Places of The Cotswolds
The Hidden Places of Dorset, Hampshire and Isle of Wight
The Hidden Places of the Lake District and Cumbria
The Hidden Places of Lancashire and Cheshire
The Hidden Places of Northumberland and Durham
The Hidden Places of North Wales
The Hidden Places of Notts, Derby and Lincolnshire
The Hidden Places of the Heart of England
The Hidden Places of the South East
The Hidden Places of South Wales
The Hidden Places of Scotland
The Hidden Places of Thames and Chilterns
The Hidden Places of Yorkshire and Humberside

Printed and bound by Guernsey Press, Channel Islands
© M & M PUBLISHING LTD
Tryfan House, Warwick Drive, Hale, Altrincham, Cheshire. WA15 9EA

Introduction

THE HIDDEN PLACES is designed to be an easily used book, taking you, in this instance, on a gentle meander through the beautiful countryside of Lancashire and Cheshire. However, our books cover many counties and now encompass most of the United Kingdom. We have combined descriptions of the well-known and enduring tourist attractions with those more secluded and as yet little known venues, easy to miss unless you know exactly where you are going.

We include hotels, inns, restaurants, various types of accommodation, historic houses, museums, gardens and general attractions throughout this fascinating area, together with our research on the local history. For each attraction there is a line drawing and a brief description of the services offered. A map at the beginning of each chapter shows you each area, with many charming line drawings of the places we found on our journey.

We do not include firm prices or award merits. We merely wish to point out *The Hidden Places* that hopefully will improve your holiday or business trip and tempt you to return. The places featured in this book will we are sure, be pleased if you mention that it was The Hidden Places which prompted you to visit.

***THE HIDDEN
PLACES OF
LANCASHIRE AND CHESHIRE***

CONTENTS

CHAPTER ONE

Greater Manchester

Bramall Hall

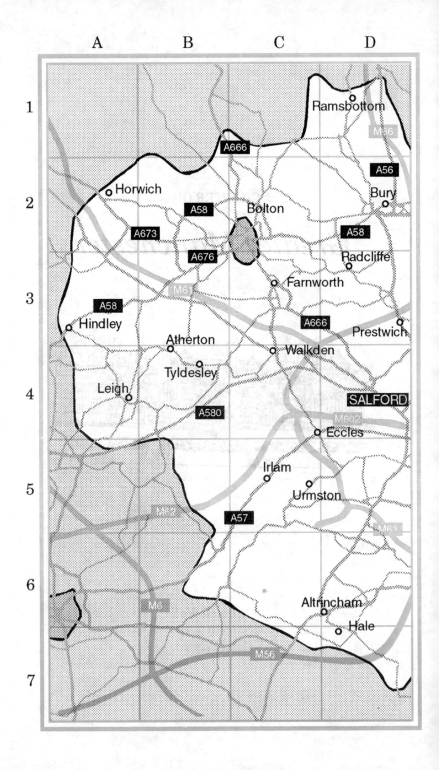

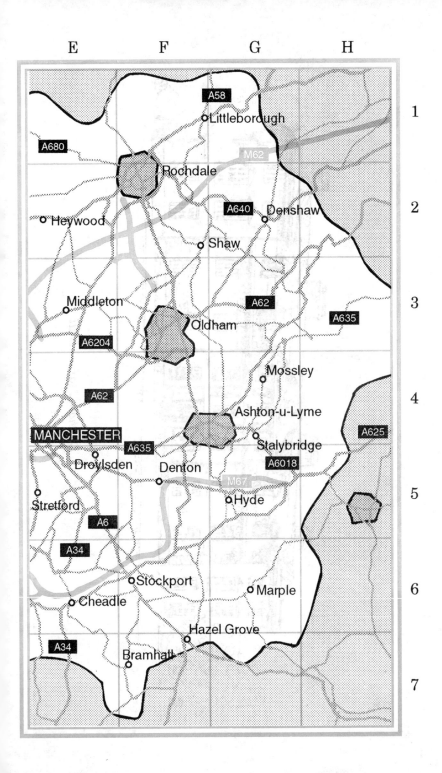

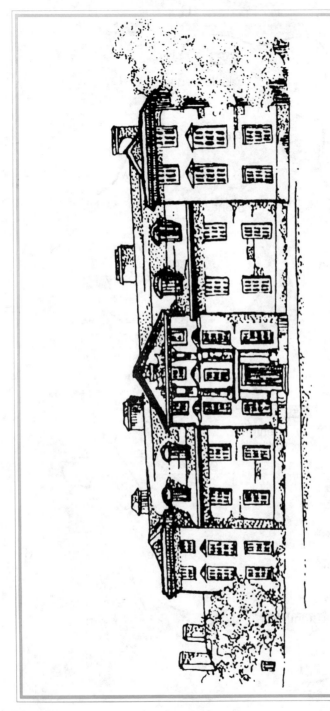

Dunham Massey Hall

CHAPTER ONE

Greater Manchester

Only a very short time ago, if anyone had suggested taking a short holiday in **Manchester**, they would have been regarded, to say the least, as eccentric. These days, however, Manchester has a thriving tourist industry and is a popular destination.

What has changed? To a degree Manchester has. The city is cleaner, brighter than it ever was in the past, with purer air, cleaner buildings, green spaces and parks where once was dereliction. It also has a new regard for its extraordinary civic and industrial heritage.

Manchester's history begins in Roman times when a small but important fort was built on the River Irwell, a tributary of the Mersey, where the road between Chester and York began its long ascent through the Pennine hills. During medieval times the town of Manchester grew in the area where the cathedral now stands and the ruined fort, Castle-in-the-field, stood abandoned in what had become a deer park.

The development of **Castlefield** began in the late 18th century when James Brindley constructed the Bridgewater Canal for the Duke of Bridgewater, to bring coal from his mines at Worsley. Later, in 1804, the Rochdale Canal was opened, connecting Manchester with Yorkshire, and the Castlefield Canal basin developed as the junction of the two.

When trains began to take over from canals, Castlefield was the site for the World's first passenger railway station. Liverpool Road Station was the terminus of the Liverpool and Manchester Railway. It was designed by rail pioneers George Stephenson and his son Robert and was opened by the Duke of Wellington.

Castlefield, just behind Deansgate, close to both Deansgate Station and the G-MEX exhibition centre, is an ideal place to start a visit to the city. The area has been redeveloped in recent years to create an urban heritage park. The trains don't run from Liverpool Street station any more, and the canals aren't used for transporting coal, but there is plenty to see and do. You can step back in time and visit the reconstructed Roman Fort on the site of the ancient fort of Mancunium or simply stroll along the renovated canal paths, perhaps pausing for a drink or a meal at one of the many canalside pubs, cafes and hotels. For further information on Castlefield ring the information line on 061 832 4244.

Manchester's most important period of history however, must surely have been the Industrial Revolution of the late 18th century.

It was the mild, moist climate of Lancashire, together with the abundant water of fast flowing Pennine streams that created an ideal environment for the spinning and weaving of cotton. As far back as the 13th century they were weaving cloth around Manchester - mainly wool. The mechanisation of the industry following the invention of Crompton's Mule and Arkwright's Spinning Jenny in the 18th century led to rapid growth of the industry, not so much in Manchester but in the rapidly growing towns and villages nearby - Bolton, Oldham, Ashton, Bury and Rochdale. Vast imports of raw cotton from the United States which came through the port of Liverpool along the Bridgewater and Leeds-Liverpool canals were balanced by equally significant exports of brightly printed fabrics to the expanding British Empire.

Manchester became the region's great trading centre, affectionately called Cottonopolis, with its Exchange fixing the price of raw cotton worldwide.

You can still visit the **Royal Exchange** where much of this trading took place in the late 19th and early 20th century, a vast handsome building between Corporation Street and St. Anne's Square. When it was no longer needed for this purpose, rather than being demolished or altered beyond recognition, it became the home of a remarkable theatre which was constructed inside the original great hall. The building still keeps its Cottonopolis flavour and character and the prices from its last day of trading remain to this day! The Royal Exchange Theatre is now a leading centre for arts in the North West. To find out what's going on, ring the box office on 061 833 9833.

Manchester's emergence into what historians describe as the world's first industrialised city was not just based on cotton. Good communications and easy access to nearby coalfields enabled it to grow rapidly as a major centre of engineering, initially forging mill engines to service the new mills, followed by steam locomotives and, as the 19th century progressed, a wide variety of heavy engineering equipment and machinery, from power stations and ship engines to aeronautics, much of it for export.

Trade was given a considerable boost in 1894 with the opening of the Manchester Ship Canal. Manchester had been under the stranglehold of the Port of Liverpool for years, having to pay heavy dues for any imports and exports passing through. This was the main reason for the decision to build the Manchester Ship Canal, an amazing feat of engineering which, at the substantial sum of £15m, turned an industrial city forty miles from the sea into a major inland port.

Coming into the twentieth century, Manchester was still at the forefront of modern technology. In the nearby suburb of Hulme, in the years after the first world war, Charles Rolls and Henry Royce manufactured their first motorcars, before moving South to Crewe and greater things. The world's first modern electronic computer was developed in the city - at the University of Manchester Institute of Science and Technology, or UMIST for short. Built in the 1950's, and in use until quite recently, it had a slower 'brain' than most of todays pocket calculators and filled a large room, weighing tons rather than ounces.

Much of the region's past can be understood from a visit to the remarkable **Museum of Science and Industry** in Manchester, which is situated in Castlefield. The museum is located in the buildings of Liverpool Road Station. In this site of international importance, the museum charts the history of the world's first industrial city.

You can see the wheels of industry turning in the Power Hall, with the largest collection of working steam mill engines in the world. The gallery also houses some of the finest locomotives ever made in Manchester, including a massive Beyer Garrett steam locomotive from South Africa Railways, made at Beyer Peacock's works in Gorton. Huge exhibits also feature in the Air and Space Gallery, which is packed with the planes that made flying history, and you can learn about cotton mills in their heyday in the Textile Gallery. The Making of Manchester explores how the city developed from Roman times to the present and Underground Manchester, an exhibition about sanitation and sewerage, contains a reconstructed Victorian sewer - complete with sounds and smells!

In addition to exploring the past the museum also looks to the future. The Out of this World space gallery explores space - fact and fiction - and visitors can learn about science while having fun in Xperiment! the hands-on science centre. The museum is open from 10 to 5 every day of the year (except over Christmas). For more details ring the 24 hour information line on 061 832 1830.

Within easy walking distance of Castlefield is **Granada Studios Tour**, the only attraction of its kind in Europe. Granada Television's headquarters are in Water Street, and the company had the brilliant idea of opening part of the studios to the public, so you can visit the set of Coronation Street, sit in a replica House of Commons bench, or discover what went on at 221B Baker Street, the residence of Mr Sherlock Holmes. You can also experience 'out of this world' cinematic adventures with Motion Master, which takes you on an exciting journey into the 21st century. There's even a Sooty show for the younger visitors and opposite the entrance, across the car park, Captain Salt (yes, that's his real name) runs cruises up and down the Irwell.

However, Manchester City Centre is more than these things. You don't have to be in the city long, whether you arrive by train (the city lies in the centre of excellent network rail services, both Inter-City and suburban) or by car (there is an excellent system of well signed off-street parking) before you begin to appreciate that you really are in a great European city. The introduction of Manchester's Metrolink, a new tram system which criss-crosses the city centre, adds to the increasingly cosmopolitan feel of the place. A superb heritage of late Victorian and early Edwardian warehouses and office blocks, some of them richly decorated and of monumental proportions, gives the narrow streets of the city centre a sense of wealth and importance which later sky-scraper office blocks cannot match.

Albert Square is an inevitable focal point. The city's magnificent Gothic **Town Hall**, designed by Alfred Waterhouse and built between 1871 - 1877 at a cost of £1 million, overlooks this now pedestrianised square named after Prince Albert, consort to Queen Victoria. Alfred Waterhouse also designed the Assize Courts, Strangeways Prison, Owen's College (now Manchester University) and the Refuge Assurance building on Oxford Road. Sculptures in Manchester have been erected in the main to commemorate famous people linked with the history of the city. There are five in Albert Square. One, of Prime Minister Gladstone, depicts movement and has earned the title "The Dancing Prime Minister". The Town Hall's richly decorated interior includes wall paintings by the Pre-Raphaelite artist Ford Madox Brown, illustrating various aspects of the history of the city. Don't miss the first floor mosaic - it is composed of industrious bees, bordered with white strands to represent the cotton industry. A hundred years later the bees reappeared on Victorian style litter bins across the city!

The Tourist Information Centre is in the Town Hall extension, the St. Peter's Square side of the Town Hall. Their phone number and those of all the other Tourist Information Centres in the region are at the back of the book.

Tucked away on Mulberry Street, only a few yards from Albert Square, is the Roman Catholic Church of St. Mary, known to many as the **'Hidden Gem'**. The church dates back to 1794, the time of the French Revolution. At first St. Mary's was in fields, surrounded by the shanty homes of the poor. As the town developed, the church became hidden by commercial buildings. Recent development however, has

Barton Arcade, Manchester

St Peter's Square, Manchester

given the church a slightly more open aspect. The exterior is lovely, but the source of the name refers to the beautiful interior.

Close by is another architectural masterpiece, the **Central Library**, one of the largest Municipal libraries in Europe. This fantastic circular building of white Portland stone, designed by the American architect Frank Lloyd Wright was opened in 1934 by King George V. Visitors are recommended to take a few minutes to venture inside and admire the great hall. The circular dome is intricately decorated and gilded and the inscription, carved in gold letters, has inspired countless readers, students and visitors:

"Wisdom is the principal thing
Therefore, get wisdom
And with thy getting get understanding
Exalt her and she shall promote thee
She shall bring thee to honour when thou dost embrace her
She shall give thy head an ornament of grace
A crown of glory shall she deliver to thee."

The basement of the library houses a small theatre, home to the Library Theatre Company. Throughout the year they produce an exciting programme of lunchtime shows, workshops, comedy, drama and world premieres. For details ring the box office on 061 236 7110.

The **Free Trade Hall** in Peter Street is the City's main concert hall where Britain's oldest professional symphony orchestra, founded in 1857 by Sir Charles Hallé, performs. It stands on a site which had a tragic association with the 1819 Peterloo massacre, where a crowd of 60,000, meeting to debate Reform in the House of Commons, were charged by local soldiers. The name commemorates Manchester's fight against the Corn Laws.

Just around the corner from here, on Windmill Street, is Manchester's **G-MEX** - Greater Manchester Exhibition and Events Centre. The building was once Central Station, opened by the Midland Railway company in 1880 and was the last of the city's railway termini to be built. Coming right into the heart of the city, its construction swept away 225 houses, home to 1200 city dwellers. The 210 foot high iron and glass arch remains as impressive today as it was the day the first train arrived. Amazingly the whole station stands on massive columns and beneath it was the goods yard and a labyrinth of warehousing. The station saw its last train in 1968 and after years as a car park was finally redeveloped as a huge exhibition centre hosting shows, concerts and trade fairs nearly every day of the week.

Straight across the road from the station is the former **Midland Hotel**, now called the Holiday Inn Crowne Plaza Midland. This monument to excess rose between 1898 and 1903 and it boasted a

Palm Court, Winter Gardens, its own Concert Hall and Theatre as well as 400 bedchambers. Outside, its walls are ornate opulence, featuring glazed brick, terracotta and polished granite, matched only by its lavish interior.

Visitors may notice a large building site on Lower Mosley Street opposite G-MEX. This will eventually be a £42m concert hall, new home for the city's internationally renowned Hallé Orchestra. The building is expected to be completed in 1996.

Close by, on Great Bridgewater Street is a unique, triangular pub, **Peveril of the Peak**. The exterior is a joy to behold, a riot of colourful glazed tiling. The interior contains a magnificently restored stained glass and wooden canopy bar. Peveril of the Peak was built in 1830 and its first licensee was a former coach driver on the London run, who named the pub after his coach.

Situated on Deansgate in Central Manchester is the **John Rylands Library**, an imposing Victorian Gothic edifice in red sandstone, a cross between a college gatehouse and a cathedral. John Rylands was a cotton merchant who became Manchester's first millionaire. He was also a devout Congregationalist, and kept a small library of theological works at his home. After his death in 1888, his widow decided to create a much larger library in his memory. The Library was to be one of the first public buildings to be lit by electricity and even had a system for filtering the dirty Manchester air. Among the many fine collections of early printed books and magnificent oriental manuscripts one treasure is a fragment of the New Testament dating back to the second century, the earliest known piece of New Testament writing in any language.

Links with old Manchester can be found in and around the city's 15th century Cathedral on Victoria Street not far from Victoria Station. Built in Perpendicular Gothic style and beautifully restored after 1940's war damage it has a wealth of delightful carvings and unusual 18th century wrought-iron rails. Located in the Cathedral is the **Manchester Cathedral** Brass Rubbing Centre. Visitors can choose from a vast selection of replicas of original brasses from English Churches.

Just across Fennel Street is the astonishing **Chetham Hospital and Library**, built on the site of a 14th century Manorial Hall, once home to the Lord of Manchester. The building contains one of England's oldest and most remarkable libraries, together with a 'bluecoat' school founded by Sir Humphrey Chetham, who left a bequest which was used in the 17th century to turn the manor house into a college for poor boys. Today Chetham's is a very well known school for gifted young musicians.

Hall i'th' Wood, Bolton

On Cheetham Hill Road, the other side of Victoria Station, is the **Manchester Jewish Museum**. Manchester has had a Jewish community for over 200 years and the museum celebrates their contribution to the city. It is housed in the former Spanish and Portuguese Synagogue and as well as a permanent display of photographs, objects and recorded memories of Jewish life early this century, there are frequent temporary exhibitions. Visitors are also welcome in the synagogue itself, restored to its original splendour with Moorish decoration and fine stained glass windows.

The city has long been a centre of learning and scholarship. Among its great men are John Dalton, the founder of atomic theory, and the physicist James Prescott Joule. Their intellectual inheritance is reflected in the two great universities - Manchester University itself on Oxford Road, and the University of Manchester Institute of Science and Technology, which together with Salford University and two large polytechnics constitute one of the largest complexes of higher education in Western Europe. The **Manchester Museum** and the splendid **Whitworth Art Gallery** form part of the University complex on Oxford Road, the latter with an outstanding collection of watercolours that balances the fine collection of old masters and Pre-Raphaelites in the City Museum on Moseley Street. Beyond the University lies Platt Fields, a pleasant park which also houses the city's Costume Museum.

With such a large student population, it is not surprising that Manchester, Britain's City of Drama in 1994, is a major cultural centre, with two large Victorian theatres, the Palace and the Opera House which take opera, ballet and touring productions, as well as the Royal Exchange Theatre and the more experimental Green Room and Contact Theatres.

The city also has a variety of jazz and folk clubs and a lively night life, and a truly cosmopolitan choice of restaurants.

Most great cities throughout the world have a **'China Town'**, and Manchester is no exception. As one would expect, a thriving oriental pot pourri of restaurants, gift shops, warehouses and banks are to be found in this small area of Manchester. The Chinese influence on the area is signified by the enormous and beautiful pagoda style archway, which is the symbolic entrance to China Town. However, there are restaurants from all parts of the Orient to be found here, including Japan, Thailand, India, Hong Kong, and all places East!

Situated in Shambles Square, **Sinclairs** stands on the original site of The Punch House, which was started by John Shaw in 1738. However, records indicate that a building has stood on this site since the 14th century. The Punch House housed the first Gentleman's Club in Manchester, and was occupied by John Shaw until his death in 1796 at the age of 83 years. Around 1845, oysters were introduced to the premises, and alcoholic beverages some 20 years later. Fifteen square yards of the site of the old Punch house is now occupied by the north-west corner of Sinclairs.

Also in Shambles Square, **The Old Wellington Inn** is one of the places where the commerce that made Manchester great began. In it lived some of the men and women who founded the City's first bank and cotton industry, and built its first quay. Also born here was the inventor of Phonetic Shorthand, John Byrom. Other inhabitants helped to found at least one City church and a hospital. The exact date of the building is unknown. A spurious date of 1328 was once displayed at the Inn, but experts now put its construction date at around 1550. Literally, the greatest upheaval the building had ever seen took place in the summer of 1971, when it was 'lifted' four feet nine inches during the construction of the Shambles Square Market Place development.

Manchester isn't just a city centre, and it is surprisingly easy to escape into fine areas of countryside, for example **Heaton Park**, reached either by road on the A576 (the link to the M62) or by the City's new high-speed Metrolink tram system to Bury. Acres of superb open countryside, a Regency house and formal gardens, boating lakes, a rare breeds centre and a restored old fashioned tramway system can all be found here.

Why not visit the **Fletcher Moss Botanical Gardens** in the southern suburb of Didsbury. The gardens and playing fields were officially given to the city early this century by the late Alderman Fletcher Moss. The location and southerly aspect of the rock gardens has made it possible to create a haven of botanical beauty. The garden contains many uncommon alpines, bulbs and shrubs as well a natural pond, orchid house and heather and wild gardens.

Much beautiful countryside lies within the satellite Metropolitan Boroughs that form the county of Greater Manchester. Including the City of Manchester itself, there are no less than ten constituent boroughs around the central core, the others being Salford, Wigan, Bolton, Bury, Rochdale, Oldham, Tameside, Stockport and Trafford. All have their special qualities and areas of individual interest.

Salford is Manchester's twin across the River Irwell. Its art gallery in Peel Park in the Crescent by the River Irwell now contains the Lowry Centre, a tribute to L.S. Lowry, the great Lancashire artist who during the 1920s and 30s meticulously recorded a now vanished scene of industrial poverty and hardship. The old Salford of Harold Brighouse's 'Hobson's Choice' and Walter Greenwood's 'Love on the

Dole' has echoes in Lowry's paintings.

Agecroft, Greater Manchester's last coal mine closed a few years ago ending a chapter of industrial history that stretches back four generations and more. The rich seam of coal spread out from the city across southern Lancashire and well within living memory there were a dozen and more pits mining it. The story of the coal field is told at **Salford Mining Museum** in Buile Hill Park off the A576. One of the mines has been preserved - Astley Green Colliery - just off the A580 East Lancashire road. It is looked after by volunteers and also provides a home for the Red Rose Live Steam Group who restore all kinds of steam engines.

The biggest change in Salford is the emergence of Salford Docks as a major tourist and residential centre. Renamed **Salford Quays**, the waterfronts now provide a backdrop to apartments, pubs and walkways, and are eventually to be served by a planned extension to the Metrolink.

At the other side of the city lies a different kind of waterway heritage, the astonishing Bridgewater Canal basin at **Worsley** (reached by bus or the A572 road from the City Centre). Here, in an area of lovely woodlands, you can see where the Duke of Bridgewater first opened his canal from his Worsley coal mines to carry coal to the centre of Manchester, in the 1760s. This new canal halved the price of coal and thus began the Industrial Revolution that helped to change the western world.

Worsley Old Hall is the ancestral home of the Duke of Bridgewater. This splendid half-timbered 16th century manor house now provides the venue for conferences, wedding receptions and extravagant Jacobean banquets, where visitors can enjoy a candlelit evening of feasting and merriment in the company of knights and fine ladies. Situated in the vaulted cellars beneath the Old Hall is The Duke's Cellar Restaurant, which with its unique structure of arched alcoves provides the perfect setting for an intimate dinner.

West of Manchester, **Bolton** is another mill town that defies expectations, its very fine Victorian town hall being the central point in a recently extensively refurbished pedestrianised shopping and leisure area with shopping malls, a restored market hall, a superb leisure centre including a swimming pool, the celebrated Octagon Theatre, and an excellent local museum.

Bolton Festival, at the end of August, is a very popular event. It runs for a whole week and there is a vast range of attractions, which include Morris Dancing and brass bands. The Victorian market is a favourite event, with everyone dressing up in full period costume.

Situated on the A673 in Bradshaw near Bolton, **The Lamb Inn** is a friendly and welcoming pub which boasts wonderful views across The Jumbles, a popular local beauty spot. This really is a traditional English pub where you can choose from a wide selection of ale and relax with your drink in the cosy atmosphere of the beamed bar. Bob and Naomi Ginnaw are lovely hosts whose warm hospitality has brought repeat visits by customers from all over the world as well as making The Lamb a popular venue with the locals. Within easy reach of many local attractions such as Turton Tower, Smithills Hall and Hall I' Th' Wood, the inn is an ideal stop-off point during a day's exploring.

The Lamb Inn, Bradshaw Road, Bradshaw, Near Bolton
Tel: 0204 852402

To the west lies **Wigan**, the town that turned a music hall joke on its head. The old canal basin on the Leeds-Liverpool Canal had a coal wharf known as **'Wigan Pier'**, jokingly referred to by George Formby, and by George Orwell in a documentary book about working-class life in the North in the 1930s. But Wigan has used the complex of old warehouses and mills around the canal basin to create a new Wigan Pier, a major leisure attraction with its own Piermaster. There are canal boat rides, and remarkable exhibitions based on local social history of "The Way We Were", with costumed actors whose activities in the reconstructed schoolroom bring back vivid memories of childhood.

Wigan isn't a town living in the past, but has a modern town centre, with fine countryside on its own doorstep such as the Douglas Valley Trail. Even Wigan's coal mining past has interesting links with the natural world - **Pennington Flash**, a large lake caused by mining subsidence, is now a wildlife reserve and country park.

The Croal-Irwell Valley to the south of Bolton now forms part of one of the great countryside success stories of recent years. From **Moses**

17

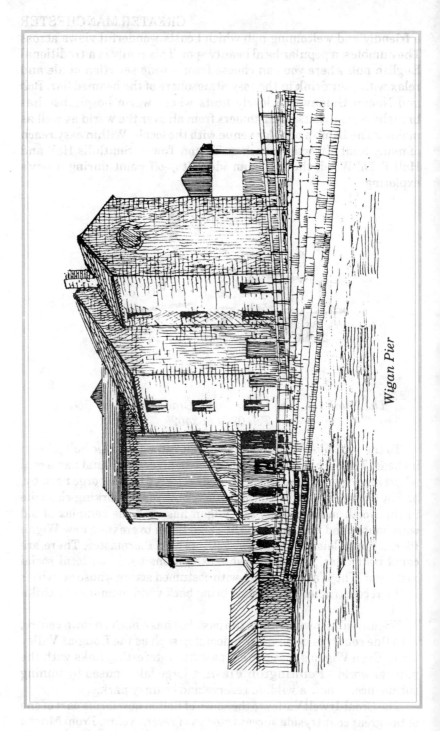

Wigan Pier

Gate Country Park southwards, a former derelict industrial valley has now been turned into a beautiful green corridor of lakes, streams, woods and walkways, supported by a lively warden and recreation service.

To the north of Bolton lie magnificent moorlands, forming the southern edge of the West Pennine Moors, through which walking opportunities abound, varying from full moorland hikes to gentle strolls. For example, there are lakeside walks in Jumbles Country Park around Jumbles reservoir, the wide open moors around Winter Hill, and the lovely open parkland around Rivington and Anglezarke Reservoirs.

You enter the village of **Rivington** across a long causeway that spans the huge two mile long reservoir, built in the 1850's to supply water to Liverpool. Half of the old village now lies beneath the water and of the remaining half only the stubby spire and weather-cock of the part-Elizabethan church are visable above the trees as you approach. Opposite the church is the village primary school, built in 1656 and just off the triangular village green is the handsome Georgian Fisher House, once home of John Fisher, who was vicar for half a century from 1763.

Rivington Hall lies at the end of a long avenue of beech trees. There has been a hall on the site since Saxon times, the present house being built by Robert Andrews in 1780. In 1900 the house was sold to soap-magnate William Lever, later Lord Leverhulme, who restored the two vast Saxon tythe barns in the grounds. Both are of cruck construction, with massive paired oaks supporting the roof and walls. They need to be big as they would have become a sort of 'Noah's Ark' during winter, sheltering the estates farm animals and all their fodder. Lord Lever-hulme had the grounds laid out as formal gardens with ponds, bridges, mock-temples, tower and hanging gardens, then threw them open to the public. He also had a replica of the long-vanished Liverpool Castle built overlooking the reservoir. The park is now gloriously overgrown and decaying, but holds a special attraction for being that. Above the park is Rivington Pike with its 18th century lookout tower and towering over everything the television mast on Winter Hill, visable from most of the north-west on a clear day.

Enjoying a secluded location surrounded by 4.5 acres of beautifully laid out gardens, the **Egerton House Hotel** lies just off the A666 at **Egerton** and provides an idyllic base for a relaxing break away from it all. Originally built over 200 years ago for a prominent local family, today it has been tastefully converted into an elegant Edwardian style hotel. All the bedrooms are en-suite and equipped to the high standard commensurate with a hotel of this calibre. The restaurant is renowned for its superb cuisine, with both à la carte and table d'hôte menus ensuring ample choice for the most discerning guest. Its elevated setting and large picture windows offer lovely views of the garden, which when floodlit in the evening enhances an air of romance. With many places of interest within easy reach from here, Egerton House Hotel makes a luxuriously comfortable holiday base.

Egerton House Hotel, Blackburn Road, Egerton Tel: 0204 307171

The fine Pennine moorland backcloth is shared with **Bury**, a town famous for its black puddings, but like Bolton enjoying an attractively refurbished town centre. One fascinating development has been the reopening of the old railway line between Bury, Ramsbottom and Rawtenstall as the East Lancashire Steam Railway. The former Bolton Street Station is now a small museum, with regular steam services through the Upper Irwell valley at weekends and during holiday times.

Rochdale has its origins in medieval times. It lies in a shallow valley formed by the little River Roch on the slopes of the Pennines, whose broad summits just above the outskirts of the town are often snow covered in winter. Another once prosperous cotton town, its handsome Town Hall rivals Manchester in style if not in size.

Rochdale, to the east of Greater Manchester, was the birthplace of both the 19th century political thinker, John Bright, and the celebrated entertainer Gracie Fields, but perhaps its chief claim to fame is with the birth of the Co-operative movement. In carefully restored Toad Lane to the north of the town centre, you'll find the world's first consumer Co-operative store, the Rochdale Pioneers. The Co-op movement now represents a staggering 700 million members in 90 countries, and the celebration of its 150th anniversary in 1994 has focused worldwide attention on the original Co-op shop on Toad Lane, now a museum.

Between Rochdale and Littleborough lies **Hollingworth Lake**, originally built as a supply reservoir for the Rochdale Canal, but for many years a popular area for recreation known colloquially as "The Weavers' Seaport", for cotton workers unable to enjoy a trip to the seaside. It is now part of the Hollingworth Lake Country Park with a fine visitor centre, and you can still enjoy trips on the lake as well as walks around its shores.

It's worth taking the A58 Halifax road from Littleborough to see the famous **Blackstone Edge Roman Road**, a stone causeway crossing this high Pennine pass. It is walkable from the roadside layby to the medieval cross, the Aigin Stone at its summit, a superb viewpoint over the entire Lancashire plain to the coast.

The great square red mills of **Oldham** still dominate the town, though many have now been put to new uses. The town, soon to be linked to central Manchester by the new Metrolink Supertram, is notable for its lively Coliseum Theatre and for its position close to superb scenery in the South Pennines and the Peak District, most notably the moorland villages of Delph, Denshaw, Dobcross and Uppermill. **Uppermill** is the largest of these and lies in the upper reaches of the Tame Valley offering lovely walks along the Huddersfield Canal with boat trips in the summer. Brownhill Visitor Centre situated just to the north of Uppermill, is an ideal starting point for a visit to Saddleworth and can provide a wide range of local information. Nearby Dovestone Reservoir, just in the Peak District National Park, is a popular sailing and birdwatching centre.

Tameside was a name coined in 1974 to describe the district which includes the towns of Stalybridge, Ashton, Hyde and Denton, and other communities which fringe onto the Cheshire Pennine border. All have pleasant town centres with much of interest. The Church of St. Michael and All Angels at **Ashton**, for example, is noted for its medieval glass, whilst St. Lawrence's at Denton has the nickname 'Th'owd peg' because reputedly neither nails nor metal were used in its construction, only wooden pegs. Situated in the centre Ashton, in the Victorian Town Hall, is the Museum of the Manchesters. Opened by the Queen mother in 1987 it tells the story of the Manchester Regiment in the context of the local community that its soldiers came from. You can discover what life was like for troops and civilians during the time of the Peterloo massacre, in the trenches of the First World War and during the Blitz. The Town Hall stands on the Market Place and the museum is open Monday to Saturday 10am to 4pm.

The Tame and Etherow Valleys, both higher tributary valleys of the River Mersey, have been kept as attractive linear green spaces and walkways through otherwise busy urban districts, and contain some lovely areas of unspoiled countryside on the edge of both the Peak District and the South Pennines.

Country lovers will discover a beautiful oasis at **Etherow Country Park**, which is situated at Compstall on the B6104 between Romiley and Marple Bridge. Once part of the estate belonging to George Andrew who built Compstall Mill in the 1820s, the park covers an area of 240 acres. A haven for ramblers and birdwatchers, the park lies at the halfway point of the Etherow-Goyt Valley Way Footpath. The Goyt Way, a ten mile trail to Whaley Bridge, also starts here. The park provides an ideal habitat for a rich variety of bird and wildlife as well as many different plant species. The nature reserve here, which is managed by Cheshire Conservation Trust, has been designated a

Site of Special Scientific Interest.

Etherow Country Park, Compstall, Stockport Tel: 061 427 6937

The Mersey Valley leads into **Stockport**, a town famed for its 700 year old market, part of which is held in a handsome Victorian market hall. The town centre is dominated by the 27 arch railway viaduct built by the Manchester & Birmingham Railway and opened in 1841. Its two tracks soon became congested and a second almost identical viaduct was built next to it in 1898, the two are so close in fact that it's hard to tell they're separate. The two structures contain 22 million bricks and are the biggest brick built structure in Europe.

The outer fringes of Stockport edge onto the green slopes of the Peak District and include towns such as Marple in the Goyt Valley, noted for the Peak Forest Canal which is part of the 100 mile Cheshire Ring.

Marple Bridge lies just north of Marple and here on Town Street you will find **Grays Café Bar**, the perfect place to call in for a refreshing cup of tea or tasty meal. Karen Thorpe is the friendly hostess who specialises in good home baking and delicious cream teas, using only the finest fresh produce. Attractive surroundings and a warm, friendly atmosphere create the perfect environment in which to savour your chosen dish from an extensive and reasonably priced menu. In addition to being open for meals during the day, the café is also open on Friday and Saturday evenings between 7.00pm and 10.00pm, bookings only, and you are invited to bring along your own wine to complement your dinner.

Stockport's potential was first recognised by the Romans, but it wasn't until the arrival of the Saxons that the town gained its name. However, there is no mention of it in the Domesday Book, the reason for this being unclear. But Stockport rose again, still under the leadership of the Normans, to claim a place in many chapters of

22

British history.

Up to the beginning of the 18th century it continued to be an attractive and prosperous market town, but all this changed with the start of the Industrial Revolution. By 1760 there were seven silk mills in the town, and the number of mills increased dramatically following the arrival of cotton spinning. Like most industrial towns of that period, Stockport had its problems, with the evolution of organisations pressing for industrial and social reform.

In 1938, prior to the outbreak of World War II, a labyrinth of passages was cut into the soft, red sandstone of Stockport town centre to provide an extensive system of underground air raid shelters. They survive today, almost intact, and you can visit them on a fascinating underground tour. You are provided with a helmet and lamp, and an expert guide will point out and explain the many interesting features: the wardens' area, toilet and washing facilities, first aid area and original bunk-beds! Tours are on the first Sunday of every month in the afternoons. For details ring 061 474 4460.

Stockport was once a great hat town, with many factories sending everything from bowlers to pith helmets all over the Empire. One of the biggest and most famous, Christies, survives to this day and is the last hatters in Britain still making traditional bowlers. Incidently the phrase 'mad as a hatter' comes from the industry's use of highly poisonous mercury for treating the felt used in the hats.

People all over the country stand on another Stockport product. Before its closure Needhams Foundry produced hundreds of thousands of cast iron man-hole covers, grids and the like, which have found their way all over the country.

Grays Café Bar, 22 Town Street, Marple Bridge Tel: 061 449 0132

Just as Rolls-Royce had humble beginnings in Manchester Jaguar cars can be said to have begun in the Stockport suburb of Woodsmoor.

23

William Walmsley began building motorcycle sidecars there before moving to Blackpool in the 1920's. In the seaside resort he met William Lyons, began full-time manufacture, expanded into building car bodies and finally complete cars; moving to Browns Lane in Coventry in 1928. The rest is, as they say, history.

One of Stockport's more unusual hidden places is strictly for gentlemen only. **The Queens Head** pub, on Great Underbank, not only has a very ornate bar and very civilised reading room, with an impressive glass skylight but also boasts having the smallest gents urinal. With standing room for one, and a pretty small one at that, it's certainly a fascinating curiousity in a very pleasant pub.

Bramall Hall, Bramall Park, Bramhall, Stockport
Tel: 061 485 3708

Just south of Stockport you will find a very special place which should feature high on your list of essential places to visit. Probably one of the finest and most attractive properties in Cheshire, **Bramall Hall** is a splendid black and white timbered manor house dating back to the 14th century. Many changes and alterations over the past 500 years mean that visitors today can admire the varying architecture, design and decoration of five centuries. Oak furniture and ornate, wood-panelled walls abound, each of the rooms having its own distinctive style and appeal, especially the Victorian Kitchens. The Great Hall with its enormous fireplace and flagstoned floor, reveals its medieval origins, although later alterations have added Tudor influences. Outside, the 70 acres of parkland provide a peaceful oasis in which to walk and watch the leisurely activities of waterfowl on the lakes and for younger members of the family, there is an enclosed play area to enjoy. The 'in-house' Gift Shop is a browser's haven, full of tempting mementos. At The Stables Café you can sample mouthwatering homemade cakes, snacks and light meals to appeal to every

24

taste.

Finally, Trafford is a borough which encompasses everything from Victorian terraces to green belt farmland, all within a few miles of the city centre. Driving down the M56 from Stockport to Chester you will pass the turn off for Manchester International Airport. A huge expanse of buildings and a recently opened second terminal give the area an unrivalled communications network, but not without controversy, as plans for a further runway are being vigorously opposed by some of the local residents.

Near here are the villages of **Hale** and Hale Barns where there is a wealth of excellent restaurants and some good hotels convenient for the airport. Tucked away, very near to the airport is the delightful **Etrop Grange** (Telephone 061 499 0500) which is a charming country house hotel, renowned for its food but almost engulfed by the ever developing airport.

In Hale itself there are no fewer than four Italian restaurants with the **San Rocco** tucked away incongruously behind Iceland! A consistent favourite. Reservations on 061 929 8024. Further up the main street, Ashley Road, the recently refurbished **Evergreen** is an elegant Chinese eatery (telephone 061 928 1222) and across the railway lines heading towards Altrincham is a local landmark, **Hale Wine Bar**. More of an institution than a mere place to eat or drink, the food is good and reasonably priced. Forget booking, as on busy nights it's standing room only.

Altrincham is a busy town and while only a few minutes from Manchester and a mere 20 minutes on the new Metrolink tram system it has retained a market town feel to it. All the major high street names are here, but there are still a good number of individually run enterprises which saves you from having that "haven't we been here before" feeling, so common now as many town and city centres have nothing but chain stores to offer the shopper. Altrincham has a busy market and some good places to eat. On The Downs, a road running from Altrincham to Bowden is the popular "**The French**" and opposite its sister restaurant "**The Brasserie**". Both offer classic french cuisine with The French being a more formal restaurant, while the Brasserie caters for more informal dining (bookings on 061 928 0808). **Francs**, tucked away on Goose Green, is also a great place to try - telephone on 061 941 3954.

Up the road in Bowden is a good family eating place called **Deckers**. It has a wide choice and very generous portions, all reasonably priced. Telephone on 061 941 5253.

Tucked away in a corner, bounded by the M56 and M6 motorways is Dunham Massey which is home to **Dunham Massey Hall** and Park.

Excellent walks can be had here and there are often craft fairs held in the hall and grounds.

Past the Hall on Paddock Lane why not stop and try **The Rope and Anchor**. There has been a pub on this site for 400 years and the present building dates back 200 years. This former coaching inn is rich in history - Cromwell even stayed here once - but visitors beware, for the cellar is haunted. The food served is good, there is a wide choice and the service is always friendly. The beers are hand-pulled cask ales and there are regular guest beers. Although open plan in layout, the pub still feels cosy and welcoming. Outside there is an all-weather barbeque and a chalet is available for functions. The garden is often used for special feature nights which are very popular.

The Rope and Anchor, Paddock Lane, Dunham Massey
Tel: 061 929 8217

Of course these are only some of the many attractions within the Greater Manchester region and it is worth exploring further before making your way across the border into East Lancashire which is where we begin the next chapter.

CHAPTER TWO

East Lancashire

Haworth Gallery, Accrington

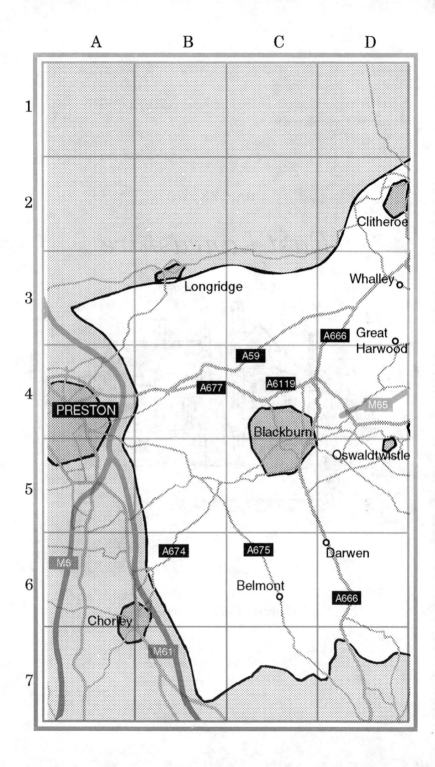

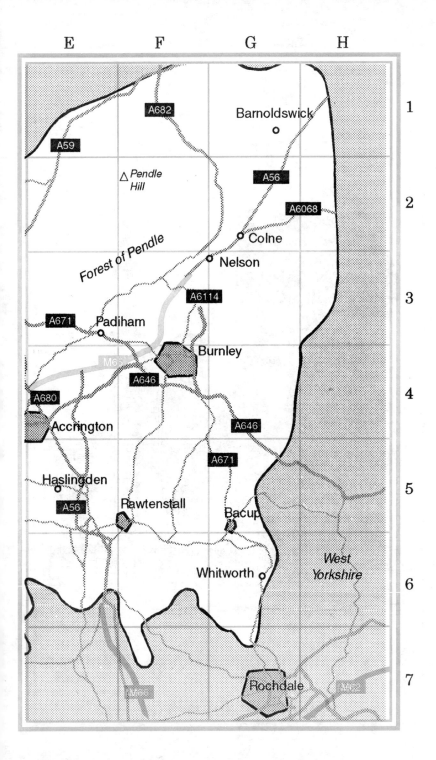

Stoneyhurst College, Hurst Green

East Lancashire

If Manchester is Cottonopolis, East Lancashire is the Cotton Capital's hinterland, a series of densely populated towns crowding into the Pennine valleys, each with its own special character and close to open moorland landscape of desolate grandeur.

Pendle Hill, that great whaleback of a mountain, dominates the northern part of this region. It is a constant feature on the skyline, giving its name to the District which includes the towns and villages on its eastern flank.

This is an area rich in legend and history - none more evocative than the tragic story of the Pendle Witches. The infamous witches were mainly old women who dabbled with plants and herbs and knew those plants that could heal and those which spelt certain death when taken. Early in the year of 1612 several people were imprisoned at Lancaster Castle. At the trial, chilling accounts of evildoings were brought to light as families and villagers accused each other. On August 20th ten women and one of their sons were found guilty and were hanged in front of huge crowds. Years later, in 1633, there were more trials. Several died in prison and four others were taken to London to be put on show.

Something of that old, dark tragedy still broods around Pendle and many memories and places which hark back to that time still remain. Find out more by visiting **Witches Galore at Newchurch** and see if you can find the grave of Alice Nutter who was hanged on that fateful day in 1612 in St. Mary's churchyard. Look up at the mysterious Eye of God carved on the tower to protect parishoners from the evil they feared lurked in the shadow of Pendle Hill.

There are many books inspired by the Witches of Pendle, you will find a good selection at Nelson Tourist Information Centre. A full list of Tourist Information Centres in the region is at the back of the book.

For all of its mysterious history, this is countryside of intimate beauty. You can take a choice of routes north of Burnley or Nelson into **Barrowford** and on to **Barley**, where there is a car park and a small Visitor's Centre and from where there is a popular, well marked path to the summit of Pendle Hill. The steep climb affords a magnificent viewpoint across to the coast and on clear days, Yorkshire's Three

Pendle Heritage Centre, Barrowford

Peaks and the Lakeland mountains beyond. There are delightful walks along the little valley formed by Pendle Water, perhaps to **White Hough** and Mistress Nutter's home - now a farmhouse - in Roughlee, or around the nearby reservoirs of Lower and Upper Black Moss, the brooding outline of Pendle Hill always a presence.

In the village of **Barley** you will find **Fox Cottage**, a cottage-style self-catering property which carries a Four Keys Commended grading and offers holidaymakers every modern comfort. Sleeping four, the cottage is attractively furnished and well-equipped throughout and outside the rear rockery garden rises to a high plateau which provides the ideal sunbathing terrace. This is one of a wide selection of properties throughout Lancashire. Elizabeth Parkinson and her staff at Red Rose Cottages would be pleased to assist in your choice - telephone 0200 27310 for a brochure.

Fox Cottage, The Bullion, Barley, Near Burnley Tel: 0200 27310

Colne is one of East Lancashire's mill and market towns, with lines of sloping grey roofs stretching along a gentle hillside above the valley formed by Colne Water. Here you'll find a monument on the main road near the War Memorial to one Wallace Hartley, who had the misfortune to be bandmaster on the Titanic in 1912. He heroically stayed at his post, conducting the band in 'Nearer my God to Thee' as the doomed liner was sinking beneath the icy Atlantic. Cobbled streets drop away steeply on either side of the main road and you can glimpse the hills above the town which quickly blend into open moorland.

For friendly, 'home from home' accommodation **Turnpike House** is ideal and situated on Keighley Road is within easy reach of the centre of Colne, but far enough away to provide a peaceful holiday base. Ann Baker is a welcoming hostess who offers very comfortable accommodation in three attractively furnished guest rooms, for which she has been awarded a One Crown Commended grading. The first thing you notice on your arrival here is the 'speaking tube', a relic from the days when this was the local doctor's house. Built during the 1820's, the house has large rooms with high ceilings and a flagstoned hallway. The south facing cottage garden is a delight to relax in and Ann is happy to provide guests with an excellent homecooked evening meal by prior arrangement.

Turnpike House, 6 Keighley Road, Colne, Lancashire
Tel: 0282 869596

To the east of Colne the moorlands rise to the bleak summits of the Pennines, but one particular hamlet is of special interest - **Wycoller**, reached either from the main A6068 Keighley road at Laneshaw Bridge, or via the mill village of Trawden.

This almost deserted Pennine village was once a thriving hand-book weaver's settlement that lost most of its inhabitants when new factories took trade away. **Wycoller Hall**, now a ruin, was the inspiration for the setting of Ferndean Manor in Charlotte Bronte's 'Jane Eyre'. The Brontes, keen walkers, would often have walked over here from Haworth. Much remains of interest in the village - a lovely old hump-backed packhorse bridge crossing Colne Water, and above the village, a single slab gritstone bridge, Clam Bridge, thought to be Iron Age in origin.

The settlement now forms part of **Wycoller Country Park**, and you must leave a car in the car park to walk a few hundred yards down the hill into the village. At Hall Barn Information Centre there are displays about village and local natural history, and a choice of easy walking trails in and around the Country Park is available.

If you are looking for peace and tranquility in the heart of beautiful Lancashire countryside, you would be well advised to seek out **Middle Beardshaw Head Farm** in **Trawden Forest** village. Turning right by the church into Burnley Road, Middle Beardshaw is the second farm on the right immediately after a sharp bend. Originally established during the 13th century as a 'vaccary' by the king of the time, this impressive farmhouse has a wonderful ambience, enhanced by exposed beams, polished parquet floors and lovely antique furniture. Bob and Ursula Mann are welcoming hosts who speak French, Italian and Spanish and provide very comfortable accommodation in four guest rooms, one boasting a four poster bed and en-suite shower. Bob also offers residential painting, walking and local history holidays for visitors looking for something a little different.

Middle Beardshaw Head Farm, Burnley Road, Trawden Forest, Lancashire

To the south is **Burnley**, a cotton town rich in history and the largest town in East Lancashire. Incorporating an area of some 50 square miles, visitors will be amazed by Burnley's wealth of contrasts, from some of the best preserved industrial landscapes in Britain, to magnificent countryside with rugged moorlands and deep gorges. The town was first established around 800AD and nestles in a basin between the River Calder and the River Brun from which it gets its name.

With the Industrial Revolution and the building of the Leeds and Liverpool Canal, Burnley grew in stature and by the end of the 19th century was the world's leading producer of cotton cloth. Take a walk along the canal towpath through the area known as the Weaver's Triangle and you step back into the 19th century. Here are to be found former spinning mills and weaving sheds; foundries where steam engines and looms were made; canal-side warehouses; domestic buildings, including a unique row of worker's houses; and a Victorian school.

The **Weavers Triangle Visitor Centre** on Manchester Road is

Chapel in a Barn, Southfield, Nr Nelson

housed in the former wharfmaster's house and canal toll office. The centre is open to the public, free of charge, on several afternoons each week during the summer months and on most bank holidays. Telephone 0282 30055 for details.

You can take a step back in time and explore history by boat as you travel along the **Leeds-Liverpool Canal**. This famous waterway cuts dramatically through Lancashire's Hill Country, from the lush farmland south of **Blackburn** to the fine summit stretch in Pendle before it strides into the Pennines. From the Weaver's Triangle the huge Burnley embankment carries the canal across the town. Known as the "straight mile", it is in fact only three quarters of a mile long, but no less exciting for that, and at sixty feet high is one of the most impressive features of the canal system. On a misty day you almost feel as if you are floating above the clouds.

Towneley Hall Art Gallery and Museums, Todmorden Road,
Burnley Tel: 0282 424213

Situated on the Todmorden Road on the outskirts of Burnley, **Towneley Hall Art Gallery and Museum** provides a fascinating and enjoyable day out for the whole family. The Hall was the home of the Towneley family from the 14th century to 1902 and parts of the present building date back to the 15th century, the oldest being the lower part of the south-east wing containing two stone spiral staircases and a Gothic window. Visitors to the Hall can explore the kitchen with its open fires on which many a banquet was cooked and then passed through to the Servants' Hall before discovering the fascinating family history in various other rooms. Towneley Park which surrounds the Hall extends to some 284 acres with facilities for golf, pitch and putt, tennis, bowls and other outdoor sports. The art collections, the Whalley Abbey Vestments and the museum of local crafts and industries, which is housed in the former brew-house and

37

laundry, are all worth visiting while you are here.

There are many charming villages around **Burnley**, each with their own particular points of interest and it is worth spending some time branching out from here along the winding country lanes and exploring some of them.

Holme Chapel is an unspoilt village situated in the beautiful Cliviger Gorge three miles south east of Burnley on the A646. The church is of particular interest and is the burial place of General Scarlett who led the charge of the Heavy Brigade at Balaclava.

There are a few old legends connected with **Cliviger**. The Towneley boggart of 'Boggart Bridge' was attributed to the restless, remorseful spirit of Sir John Towneley who enclosed 194 acres of land illegally, and forcibly ejected local tenants. The Holme too is said to be haunted.

Between Burnley and Brierfield is the parish of **Reedley Hallows**. It is a place with historic connections. Old Chattox, one of the Lancashire witches, had associations with Greenhead Farm, and Laund House was the home of John and Robert Nutter, Catholic priests who were persecuted in the 16th century.

The Oaks Hotel, Colne Road, Reedley, Near Burnley
Tel: 0282 414141

If you are looking for somewhere special to stay, the **Oaks Hotel** in Reedley stands in four acres of well laid out grounds and has a distinct air of opulence and grandeur. This impressive Victorian mansion lies close to the Pendle Forest and offers the discerning visitor a luxurious holiday base. Originally the home of Alderman Abraham Altham, a Manchester tea and coffee merchant who built the house to his own very high specifications, careful refurbishment and extension over the years has not detracted from the Oaks' individual character and charm. All of the 56 guest rooms and suites are equipped for maximum comfort, some boasting four poster beds,

38

and all with ensuite facilities. As with the rest of the Hotel, the furnishings are of the highest quality, in keeping with the age of the building. In the main lounge, splendid leather Chesterfield sofas complement perfectly the magnificent carved oak staircase and stained glass windows, above which can be seen the coats of arms of all the main local towns. This air of discreet elegance pervades throughout, from the Library Lounge and Authors Bar, to the Quills Restaurant, where you can savour the finest gourmet cuisine, accompanied by a carefully selected wine list. Whether for business or pleasure, a stay at the Oaks Hotel is sure to be memorable and one you will want to repeat.

To the west of Burnley, the township of **Padiham**, with its narrow winding lanes and cobbled alleyways, still retains characteristics of the early Industrial Revolution. It existed well before the Norman Conquest and was a market town where produce from Pendleside was bought and sold.

For lovers of historic houses, one place well worth visiting while you are in the area is **Gawthorpe Hall**. Situated on the eastern outskirts of Padiham on the edge of the Pennines, this splendid 17th century house was restored to Victorian elegance by Sir Charles Barry during the 1850s. The present house was started in 1600, but Gawthorpe had been the home of the Shuttleworth family for 200 years prior to this. Beautiful period furnishings are enhanced by ornately decorated ceilings and original wood panelled walls, providing the perfect setting for the nationally important Kay-Shuttleworth collections of needlework and lace. The Hall also houses a major collection of 17th century portraits on loan from the National Portrait Gallery. The lovely gardens surrounding the Hall are open all year round and in the shop you will find a range of quality goods providing you with the ideal memento of your visit.

Gawthorpe Hall, Padiham, Near Burnley Tel: 0282 778511

The nearby village of **Huncoat** is one of only a few local places listed in the Domesday Book and in 1986 celebrated its 900th year. The nucleus of the old village can be seen at Town Gate, together with the village stocks which have existed since 1722. It was in this same year that local man John Hacking invented the cotton carding engine.

Of further historic interest, situated off Burnley Road, Huncoat Hall is of medieval origin, and the King's Highway is the ancient road to Manchester used by John Wesley.

The unusually named village of **Fence** is not far away to the north-east of Padiham. The name of this small settlement strung out along the fields of Pendleside recalls the enclosure in which stags were kept when hunting was abandoned in Pendle Forest. At Fence Gate, there is a Slate Age Craft Centre, situated in a converted farm building now used for the manufacture of slate giftware. There has been a slate craft centre here for 22 years. Visitors can look around the workshops and visit the craft shop. Admission is free.

Lower White Lee Farm, Barrowford Road, Fence, Burnley, Lancashire Tel: 0282 613563

Fence-in-Pendle dates from the time of William the Conqueror and it is in this delightful village, set in 200 acres of rolling farmland, that you will find Lower **White Lee Farm**, a working dairy farm which is a member of the Farm Holiday Bureau. This impressive Grade II listed 18th century farmhouse provides a very comfortable holiday base and Helen Boothman is a friendly and welcoming hostess. Awarded a One Crown Commended grading by the English Tourist Board, the guest rooms are spacious and well-equipped and period furnishings throughout enhance the age and character of this lovely farmhouse. Guests have their own TV lounge to relax in as well as a separate dining room and evening meals are available by prior arrangement. There are many attractions within easy reach and of

40

course it is not far from here to Pendle, home of the famous Lancashire Witches.

Another delightful Pendle village is nearby **Higham**. Higham has been associated with Jonal Moore of White Lea, mathematician Surveyor-General of Ordnance and co-founder of the Greenwich Observatory. Keep an eye out for the Four Alls Inn. The sign outside bears four pictures and the legends: "I govern all" next to the king, "I pray for all" next to the clergyman, "I fight for all" next to the soldier, and finishes with a rather rueful looking worker and the words: "I pay far all".

Sabden is set beneath the impressive Pendle Hill, only a mile or so from Higham. Here George Fox, founder of the Quakers, had a vision which led to the foundation of that movement. The local handloom weavers of old were said to weave parkin using oatmeal as the warp and treacle as the weft! Now it is possible to visit the Sabden Treacle Mines to meet the small furry treacle miners, who are soon to be immortalised in a children's television series.

Pendle Antique Centre is another popular attraction, housed in an old mill. The centre has a constantly changing stock of antique furniture and bric-a-brac from British and European sources, most of which are refurbished on the premises.

Back towards Burnley, and travelling south on the A682 brings you to the quaintly named village of **Loveclough**, situated just on the edge of the Rossendale Valley.

Loveclough Cottage, 1302 Burnley Road, Loveclough, Rossendale
Tel: 0204 852402

Self-catering enthusiasts will find an excellent holiday base at **"Loveclough Cottage"**, a traditional Lancashire stone-built terraced cottage owned by the proprietors of The Lamb Inn in nearby Bradshaw. Attractively furnished in traditional style the cottage provides

41

very cosy accommodation, sleeping up to four people in one twin and one double room, with full central heating, a large lounge with colour TV, kitchen/dining room and telephone. To the rear there are lovely views of Goodshaw Hill and its delightful location puts "Loveclough Cottage" within easy reach of many local attractions including a nearby trout fishing lodge and "The Rossendale Way".

The area of **Rossendale** is one the most picturesque, varied and interesting areas of Lancashire's Hill Country. Nestling in the unspoilt beauty of the Irwell Valley, the market towns of Rawtenstall, Haslingden and Bacup are time capsules from Britain's industrial past.

In **Rawtenstall** visitors can discover the **Weavers' Cottage**. The building was purpose built for hand loom weaving in 1780 and is one of the last remaining buildings of its kind. It is open to the public every Saturday and Sunday, between 2 and 5, April to September.

Look out for the Newchurch Tunnels - an impressive symbol of the determination of Victorian railway companies and their engineers to overcome obstacles in the pursuit of business and profit. These tunnels were built in 1857 to take the line from Rawtenstall to Bacup through the narrowest part of the Irwell Gorge.

Not far outside Rawtenstall is **Ski Rossendale**, the North West's premier ski centre, open all year round - whatever the weather! The centre is ideal for beginners and experts alike, and tuition is available. Adjacent to Ski Rossendale is Whitaker Park andRossendale Museum.

Rossendale Museum is housed in a Victorian mill owners' mansion formerly known as Oakhill. There are impressive collections of natural history, fine art and furniture, ceramics and local industrial and domestic bygones. The extensive grounds of Whitaker Park contain something for everyone, including a bowling green, tennis courts, playground area, aviary and domestic animal enclosure. You could also enjoy a stroll amid the pleasant and well kept gardens.

At one end of the town, you will find a new railway station marking the end of a very old railway - the **East Lancashire Railway**. The original line opened in 1846 and ran until 1980 when the last coal train went to Rawtenstall. Seven years later, and with plenty of hard work and dedication from the East Lancashire Railway Preservation Society, the railway began to carry passengers again. The steam trains offer an enthralling 17 mile round trip along the River Irwell, between Rawtenstall and Bury via the picturesque market town of Ramsbottom. Trains run every weekend, with additional services in the summer. Ask at Tourist information Centres for more details.

One of the gems of East Lancashire can be found on Bank Street

Turton Tower, Chapeltown, Nr Blackburn

in Rawtenstall. **Herbal Health** is the last temperance bar in Britain. It was once part of a chain that spread throughout the cotton towns of Lancashire and was originally called Fitzpatricks. It stayed in the same family until Bob and Beryl Waddington took it over twelve years ago. The cordials and tonics were devised by the previous owners' father, back in the 1890's, and passed it on the Bob - at a price. As with any bar, there is a good choice of brews, tipples including black beer with either raisin, lemon or orange, sasparilla, blood red tonic, cream soda and dandelion and burdock - all made on the premises. Sampling the brews is only part of the Herbal Health experience, as they are a proper health shop as well, selling every medicinal herb and vitamin you can think of, many in huge jars that line a wall. The shop hasn't changed in sixty years and is a real piece of living history that you shouldn't miss. Open Monday to Saturday (except Tuesdays), 9am to 5pm.

Situated on Holcombe Road, **Helmshore**, the fascinating **Helmshore Textile Museums** offer the opportunity to discover Lancashire's Textile Heritage. Re-live the nostalgia and visit the historical working museum with demonstrations of machinery, a magnificent water wheel and Hargreaves' Spinning Jenny. There is a wonderful museum shop where you can but a momento of your visit.

To the East is the town of Bacup. Built in the 19th century for the single minded purpose of cotton manufacture, Bacup is perhaps the best remaining example of a 19th century cotton town in England. Strolling through the town centre you will discover beautifully re-stored homes and shops, the grander homes of mill owners and elegant commercial and municipal buildings hint at Bacup's proud and productive past.

Back towards Pendle Hill, and a town that few visitors wish to miss is **Whalley,** with its grey ruined Cistercian Abbey, founded in 1296 and rich in historic and architectural interest. The grounds are open to the public. The town of Whalley itself has great character and charm, and lanes link it to the village of Sabden, from where a steep and scenic pass crosses Nick o' Pendle, a notable viewpoint and hair-raising descent towards Pendleton, Clitheroe and the Ribble Valley.

Look out for Whalley Viaduct, a major landscape feature more than 600 metres long and up to 21 metres high. There are 48 arches in total, and the viaduct is built of 7 million bricks, all made locally. It was built to carry the Blackburn-Clitheroe railway line across the Calder Valley in 1850. Where it crosses the lane to Whalley Abbey, three of the arches have been given Gothic details to harmonise with the nearby 14th century gatehouse.

One of the oldest properties in Whalley, the **Toby Jug Tea Shop** (a grade 2 listed building) is over 300 years old, and is little changed externally. Inside oak beams and panelling from the nearby 13th century Cistercian Abbey are testimony to the antiquity of this the Ireland's family home.

Since opening in 1985 it has gained a reputation for the delicious home-made cakes and scones, special soups, freshly prepared sandwiches, and complimentary seasonal salads. Good wheelchair access. No smoking please! Open Wednesday, Thursday, Friday 10.00 to 4.30, Saturday, Sunday and Bank Holidays 10.30 to 5.00.

The Toby Jug Tea Shop, 20 King Street, Whalley, Lancashire
Tel: 0254 823298.

The picturesque village of **Hurst Green** lies to the west of Whalley on the main B6243 and is celebrated for Stonyhurst, its famous Roman Catholic public school. the magnificent buildings are set in extensive parkland with two huge ponds which were excavated in 1696. Cromwell stayed here in 1648 and in 1811 the building became the first public building to be lit by gas. Sir Arthur Conan Doyle is among the famous ex-scholars of the college. Stoneyhurst is open to the public on certain days of the year and tours of the building can be arranged.

In the centre of the village, **The Shireburn Arms** is a superb Hotel and Restaurant owned and personally run by Steven Alcock and his family. The emphasis here is clearly on customer satisfaction and nothing is too much trouble. Whether you come here for a tasty bar meal, a magnificent dinner in the silver service restaurant or a longer stay, you are assured of first class service in an atmosphere of friendly hospitality. Awarded Two Stars by the AA, Three Stars by the RAC and a Four Crowns grading by the English Tourist Board, you know the standard of facilities you can expect. All sixteen of the well-appointed guest rooms are en-suite and equipped for maximum

Packhorse Bridge, near Hurst Green

comfort. There are monthly wine promotions and t. a monthly public dance providing added attractions for here.

The Shireburn Arms, Hurst Green, Whalley, Near Blackburn Tel: 0254 826518

A litte further to the west is **Ribchester**. This ancient riverside village is built on the site of the Roman station of Bremetennacum. Estimated to have covered six acres of ground, a large portion of the remains lie under the old church and churchyard. The Roman Museum has recently been extended and provides interesting displays about Roman life in the area. The **Museum of Childhood** contains a wonderful collection of toys, models, dolls, doll's houses, miniatures and curios including a 20 piece working model fairground. The museum has twice been voted best small attraction in the North West.

The White Bull, Church Street, Ribchester Tel: 0254 878303

The **White Bull** can be found in the heart of Ribchester near the

Bath House and Roman Museum. Originally built and used as the local courthouse, the exact date of building is not known although the 1707 datestone was placed after an early rebuilding. The pub has an imposing porch supported by Roman pillars that were salvaged from the River Ribble. The cosy, but open interior has a lounge bar with the locals' snug off to one side and the dining room to the other. The varied menu is available in the bar and dining areas and The White Bull is famous for its casseroles, stews and fish dishes. There is a selection of unique exciting specials which are changed regularly and there is always a guest cask ale. there are open fires throughout and a fox going through the wall complements the unusual but traditional decor. There is a beer garden to the rear. Families are most welcome and the pub offers a seperate menu for children.

Lying further south, **Blackburn** is the largest town in East Lancashire, notable for its modern shopping malls, its Market Hall, its celebrated three day market, its modern cathedral incorporating the nave of the 1826 building, and Thwaites Brewery, one of the largest independent brewers of real ale in the North.

Other points of interest in this busy market town are **The Lewis Textile Museum** which is dedicated to the cotton industry and **The Museum and Art Gallery**, appropriately situated in Museum Street, which has among its many treasures eight paintings by Turner, the Hart collection of medieval manuscripts, an outstanding collection of Japanese prints and antiques, and the finest collection of Eastern European Icons in Britain.

A little to the west, about half way between Blackburn and Preston is the charming and much acclaimed parish of **Hoghton**. Undoubtedly one of the most celebrated buildings in English History, the stately home of **Hoghton Tower** is where, legend has it, King James I made his celebrated knighting of a particularly delicious joint of beef, with the eternal phrase 'I dub thee Sir Loin'! An Inn within the parish was promptly named after the event and still stands today.

Before leaving this south-eastern corner of Lancashire, it is worth also visiting **Accrington**, the principle town of Hyndburn. It has an outstanding Victorian town centre and is now a conservation area based on a splendid market hall and traditional shops. There is also a popular policy of free parking for all and the new road network has made it easily accessible by car.

Accrington is home to one of the most attractive art galleries in the North of England. **Haworth Art Gallery** is set in beautiful parkland and houses the largest collection - 130 pieces - of Tiffany Glass in Europe. The collection was presented to the town by Joseph Briggs, an Accrington man, who went to New York to work with Louis Tiffany for almost forty years. Having joined the Tiffany studios in 1890, his rise through the company ranks was swift and he soon became a foreman and then manager of the Mosaic Department. Later he held the prestigious post of Art Director and Personal Assistant to Louis Tiffany himself.

As the fashion for Tiffany Glass waned after the First World War, Louis Tiffany became despondent and concentrated his efforts on the development of an art school at Laurelton Hall, where students could learn about his personal concept of beauty. In 1924 Tiffany handed over the studios to his two managers, Douglas Nash and Joseph Briggs. The stranglehold of the economic depression in the 1920s and changing tastes and fashions eventually forced the closure of Tiffany Glass. Douglas Nash bought the Corona Glass Works and continued trading under his own name, so Joseph Briggs was left with the sad task of trying to sell off the remainder of Tiffany stock. He returned to his native Accrington in 1933, bringing his collection of Tiffany Glass with him, half of which he gave to the town, whilst the rest he distributed amongst his family. Today, visitors to the Haworth Art Gallery can view this stunning collection and learn the fascinating history behind it.

Having explored some of the fascinating towns and villages of East Lancashire, we now make our way into the next chapter by travelling north to the beautiful area of the Forest of Bowland.

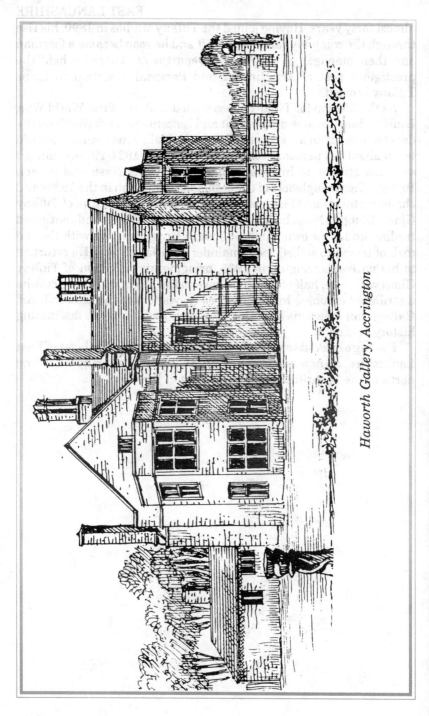

Haworth Gallery, Accrington

CHAPTER THREE

The Forest of Bowland

Slaidburn Bridge

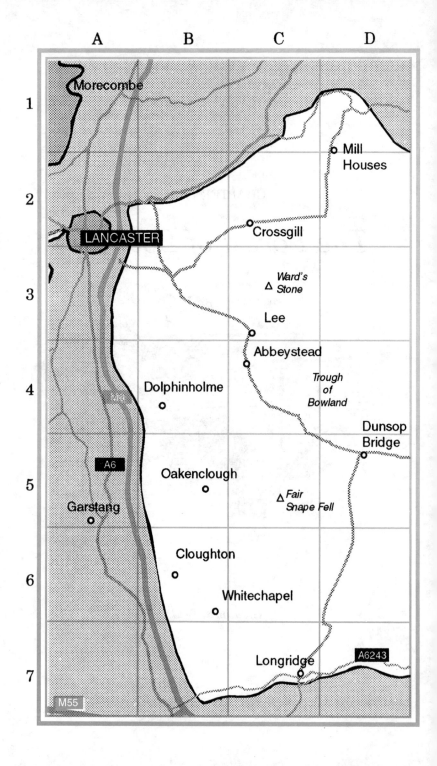

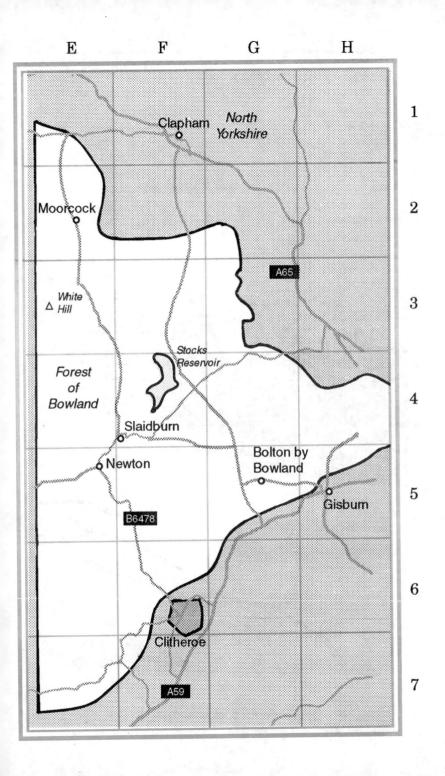

Forest of Bowland

CHAPTER THREE

The Forest of Bowland

Extending across the northern half of Lancashire, the **Forest of Bowland** is a region of scenic splendour. Designated an Area of Outstanding Natural Beauty in February 1964, this is a veritable paradise for walkers and country lovers, dotted with picturesque villages.

The eleventh largest of such designated areas, The Forest of Bowland is situated mainly in the county of Lancashire, although part of the area does extend into North Yorkshire. Somewhat a misnomer, the term "forest" derives from the latin "foris" which was formerly used to denote a royal hunting ground, an unenclosed tract of land, rather than a distinct wooded area. Its present landscape provides numerous clues to its past history. The remains of a Roman road can be clearly seen from the viewpoint at Jeffrey Hill on Longridge Fell and further clues are provided in the village names. Names such as Grindleton, Waddington, Caton and West Bradford date back to the Saxon period and Norse names are also common, such as "beck" (meaning stream) or "laithe" (meaning barn).

During the 13th century Cistercian Monks travelled from Fountains Abbey in Yorkshire and settled at **Sawley**, just to the north of Clitheroe. They toiled for years building the abbey, clearing trees and cultivating the land to grow crops. Ridge and furrow cultivation patterns can still be seen today. The influence of the Monks reached across the whole landscape of Bowland through their clearance of land for farming sheep.

The 18th and 19th centuries saw the enclosure of land by drystone walls and hedgerows. Industrial activities also influenced the landscape with stone quarries, lead, and silver mines being developed. Lime was produced locally, burnt in kilns and after crushing, spread on the farmland to improve soil fertility.

The protected status of the area means it is a real haven for a wide diversity of animal, bird and plant life. Controlled burning maintains a healthy heather moor and a good grouse population. This plays a particularly important role in the preservation of the threatened Hen Harrier, a rare bird of prey which requires substantial tracts of undisturbed heather moorland and feeds partly on grouse, of which there is a plentiful supply. Traditional field borders such as hawthorn, blackthorn, crab apple, holly and other shrubs, rising up to the levels of traditional drystone walls on the higher fells, help to maintain this natural, unspoilt picture. If you want a taste of nature at her finest, this really is the place to come.

The Forest of Bowland was chosen as one of the first places in the country to develop a chain of camping and bunkhouse barns, and there are now five Youth Hostel Association camping barns available in the Forest of Bowland. Bookings should be made in advance. Ring the Bowland Barns Reservation Office on 0200 28366.

Perhaps the most celebrated of the many routes across Bowland is the minor road from Lancaster to Clitheroe which crosses the Abbey-dale Moors and the Trough of Bowland before descending into the lovely Hodder Valley around Dunsop Bridge. This is a popular road in summer months, with most lay-bys and parking places filled as people pause to take in the breathtaking moorland views.

The old stone town of **Clitheroe** is the capital of the Forest of Bowland. Like Lancaster, it too is dominated by an 800-year-old castle on the hill, set on a limestone crag high above the little town. Little more than a ruin in a small park, when you stand inside the keep, hidden voices relate aspects of the castle's history with suitable sound effects. The **Castle Museum** has collections of local geology and history, including a clogger's workshop, a printer's shop and a lead mine.

The town's narrow, winding streets are full of character. You'll find old pubs and shops, narrow alleyways and steps, an excellent Tourist Information Centre, and the Old Grammar School. An unusual feature is the Civic Hall Cinema, an unspoiled 1920s cinema lined in plush velvet, which still has the grand piano used to accompany silent movies. It is still in use as the town cinema.

The Edisford Picnic Area can be found just outside of Clitheroe. Once a battle ground between the Scots and the Normans, this is now a pleasant family area on the banks of the river, with a miniature railway, children's play area, cafeteria and pitch and putt course.

South of Clitheroe on the B6246 is **Great Mitton**, a particularly attractive village. Until 1974 Great Mitton, with its church, was in Yorkshire, but the other part of the village, Little Mitton, divided by the River Ribble, lay in Lancashire.

The tiny hamlet of Mitton is situated on a limestone rise above the River Ribble near to its junction with the Hodder. The 13th century Church of All Hallows has the Shireburn Chapel with effigies of members of that family, sculpted by William Stanton, one of the foremost sculptors of his period. The Chancel Screen that came from

Clitheroe Castle

Sawley Abbey is also an interesting feature.

A sweeping drive leads to **Mitton Hall**, which is a stone's throw from the medieval church at Mitton. This imposing Manor House, with stately mullioned windows, was built for a cousin of Henry VII in about 1514. It stands in woodland surroundings extending to nearly 18 acres in all, with the River Ribble flowing by. Today, Mitton Hall houses a restaurant, country tavern and lodgings, telephone 0254 86544 for details.

If you go eastwards from Clitheroe, you will reach **Pendle Hill** and the villages in and around its western slopes, including Downham, one of the most attractive villages of all in a region of exceptionally fine villages.

Downham was purchased by the Assheton family in 1558, along with Whalley Abbey and is one of the loveliest villages in Lancashire. It has been maintained in virtually its original condition by the Assheton family. The present squire, Lord Clitheroe of Downham, still refuses to permit the skyline to be spoilt by TV aerials, satellite dishes or even dormer windows, which are all strictly prohibited. Because the village is so unspoilt it is often used in period films. 'Whistle Down the Wind' was filmed here. Don't miss the toilets in the car park, they have won several awards!

The church tower is a splendid example of 15th century architecture.

The Assheton Arms, Downham, near Clitheroe Tel: 0200 441227

Situated off the A59 in the middle of Downham village, opposite the church is **The Assheton Arms**. There are records of licenced premises on this site going back to 1399, however the present building only dates as far back as 1765. Look out for the initials carved over the stone fireplace, they are believed to be those of the original builder. The pub has a very olde-worlde feel to it, with low ceilings, exposed

58

beams and open fires. The Assheton Arms has an excellent reputation for food and the menu is extensive and impressive. The ales are traditional and all hand-pulled. If you happen to notice the wooden busts of guardsmen wearing 'busby' hats, they are in fact newel posts from the Busby family's department store, which later became Debenhams in Bradford.

Carrying on to the East you will reach **Rimmington**. Delightful countryside is to be found here and at the adjoining hamlets of Stopper Lane, Martin Top, Newby, Middop and Howgill. This area was the home for many years of Francis Duckworth, the famous composer of hymn tunes, including one called 'Rimmington"

Self-catering visitors will discover an idyllic holiday base at **Raikes Barn**, a superb 18th century barn conversion which carries the prestigious Four Keys Highly Commended rating. Sleeping six, the facilities, furnishings and decoration throughout are outstanding, as are the magnificent views towards Pendle Hill and the Forest of Bowland. This is one of a wide selection of properties throughout Lancashire managed by Elizabeth Parkinson and her staff at Red Rose Cottages. Telephone 0200 27310 for a brochure.

Raikes Barn, Rimington, Near Clitheroe Tel: 0200 27310

Just the other side of the River Ribble is **Bolton-by-Bowland**, a tranquil village with village green, stone cross and old stocks. The church has many ornamental carvings and a tomb dating from 1500 which has the arms of Pudsey, Percy Tempest, Hammerton and other families. The famous Pudsey tomb has an engraved figure of Sir Ralph Pudsey in full armour with the figures of his three wives and 25 children.

The Copy Nook Hotel in Bolton-by-Bowland has recently been bought by Brendan and Ruth Woods. Both Brendan and Ruth gained their experience at Ye Horns Inn at Goosnargh, owned by Brendan's

Slaidburn Bridge

parents and with an excellent reputation. In the short time Brendan and Ruth have been at The Copy Nook, they have established a name in their own right. Formerly a farmhouse, the building has been converted into a pub and restaurant with separate function room. There are also 5 en-suite bedrooms which recently been refurbished to a very high standard (available from May 1994).

Copy Nook Hotel, Bolton-by-Bowland, Clitheroe Tel: 0200 447205

The pub has a traditional country feel and the stone walls and old wooden beams add to the atmosphere. The restaurant provides excellent food with an extensive wine list.

A few miles from here is Sawley. This pleasant village is chiefly renowned for the ruins of **Salley Abbey**, a Cistercian Abbey founded by William de Percy in 1147.

A little to the east is **West Bradford**, a village with a long history of rugged independence. A stream runs deep alongside the road through the bottom half of the village and access to the houses bordering the beck is by means of quaint stone bridges.

In West Bradford you will find the traditional 400-year old English Village pub, **The Three Millstones**. Complete with low beamed ceilings, open fires and a wealth of antique furniture and brasses, this former coaching inn is a must for visitors to the area. There is even a resident ghost - a former highwayman known as Kirkham Jack. The candlelit restaurant seats 32 and has an interesting and varied menu featuring smoked oysters, fresh fish and the famous sticky toffee pudding. There is a separate bar menu offering Mediterranean style toasties and a selection of sandwiches. There are two rooms available offering bed and breakfast, and golfing breaks can be arranged.

The next village is **Waddington**, one of the Ribble Valley's best known villages, and the attractive Coronation Gardens have appeared on many a postcard and even on biscuit tins. King Henry VI

(Henry the Good) lived for a year, in secret, at Waddington Hall before being betrayed to the Yorkists. He allegedly escaped via a secret panel and staircase from the dining room, only to be captured at Brungerly Bridge, down river near Clitheroe.

The Three Millstones, West Bradford, Near Clitheroe
Tel: 0200 23340

In this quiet village you will discover an excellent holiday base at **Peter Barn Country House**, the delightful home of Jean and Gordon Smith. Originally a tythe barn, sympathetic conversion and refurbishment by the Smiths some sixteen years ago has created a house full of character and charm. For the past three years, the upper floor has been left for the exclusive use of Jean and Gordon's many guests and comprises a spacious, beautifully furnished sitting room, complete with log fire and wonderful views of the Japanese style garden plus three lovely guest rooms and a bathroom. Known locally as Rabbit Lane, the official address is Cross Lane, but evidence of Peter Rabbit abounds throughout the house and guests here will find this is one place they will return to time and again. Bed and breakfast from £17.00.

Peter Barn Country House, Cross Lane, Waddington
Tel: 0200 28585

Situated on Waddington Fell, **The Moorcock Inn** is a famous old inn with comfortable lounge bars, superb ballroom, a cosy restaurant, and seven elegantly furnished bedrooms, each with private bathrooms. The original building on this site was a farm and an alehouse built in 1831 now under ownership of Peter and Susan Fillary.

The restaurant is open for à la carte dinner every evening, and the menu includes house specialities such as fresh fish and game dishes.

Other dishes include steaks and poultry. Susan personally supervises the preparation of food and this is reflected by the way the menu changes with each passing season. Wherever possible, fresh local produce is used. Home cooked meals are served in the bar at lunchtimes and evenings, and the range of food available is extensive.

The ballroom at Moorcock makes it an ideal venue for special occasions such as wedding receptions, dinner dances and private parties. During the summer months, the gardens are used for such events, and this proves to be ideal with the backdrop of the Ribble Valley and Pendle Hill.

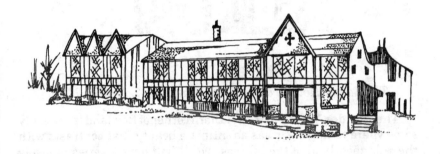

The Moorcock Inn, Fell Road, Waddington, near Clitheroe Tel: 0200 22333

Chipping is a picturesque village on the slopes above the River Loud to the north of the town of Longridge. In Medieval days no less than five watermills were sited along Chipping beck. Several attractive inns are to found in the centre one of which is the **Sun Inn**, to which there is a legend. Lizzy Dean was a serving wench at the Sun Inn, engaged to be married to a local man. On the morning of her wedding, on hearing the church bells, she looked out of the window of her room in the Sun Inn and saw her bridegroom leaving the church with another bride on his arm. She hanged herself in the attic of the pub. Her last request was that her grave be dug in the path of the church so that her ex-boyfriend had to walk over it every Sunday. She died in 1835 aged 20 and is said to still haunt the Sun Inn.

In the centre of Chipping, in the heart of the Forest of Bowland, and on the west side of the Hodder Valley, you will find a former coaching inn, **The Talbot Hotel**. The Talbot's claim to fame is that they have a resident ghost here. It isn't actually seen, but there is a distinct smell of lavender whenever it is around! The pub has recently been refurbished but the original beams have been retained throughout. There is a separate restaurant area although the same menu is available in the bar area as well. The food offered is varied and there are additional daily specials. There is a garden to the rear which is very peaceful and has a pretty stream running through it.

The Talbot Hotel, Talbot Street, Chipping Tel: 0995 61260

The **Hodder Valley** in the southern corner of Bowland is certainly somewhere to linger - it has an intimate beauty that contrasts with the wild moorland of the hilltops. You'll find here a series of lovely villages. Whitewell is known locally as 'Little Switzerland' because of its location in a deep, wooded valley. A church, an Inn and a few cottages grace this very attractive spot. **Dunsop Bridge**, a little further along the valley has been officially declared by Ordnance Survey to be the nearest village to the exact centre of the British Isles and its associated islands. How do they work these things out?

The Parkers Arms, Newton-in-Bowland, Near Clitheroe
Tel: 0200 446236

The best way to approach the next village of **Newton-in-Bowland** is said to be from the south over Waddington Fell. The views are breathtaking. John Bright the Quaker spent two years of his early life here.

Enjoying a pleasant location with wonderful views, on the hill just below Newton village, **The Parkers Arms** with its impressive black and white frontage, is a charming and traditional country pub. Originally the stables for Newton Hall, it is full of character, with open fires, oak beams and stuffed birds all enhancing a cosy, country atmosphere. In the warm, welcoming ambience of the bar you can choose from a selection of hand-pulled ales and in the comfortable beamed restaurant, an imaginative and varied menu tempts the most discerning palate. For guests seeking a bed for the night, there are also three attractively furnished guest rooms, each equipped with a TV, hairdryer and hot drinks facilities.

Just a few miles from Newton lies **Slaidburn**, a compact village with a fine 15th century church, notable for its great three-decker pulpit and unusual Jacobean chancel screen. The village has rows of cottages that indicate its links with weaving, and a famous pub, the **Hark to Bounty**. This splendid inn dates back to the 13th century and until 1895 was known as The Dog. Apparently the squire of the village, who was also the parson, had a pack of hounds: one day while out hunting, he and his party called at the inn for refreshments. Their drinking was disturbed by loud and prolonged baying from the pack outside and high above the noise could be heard the squire's favourite hound, which prompted him to call out "Hark to Bounty".

The inn also housed the ancient Moot Courtroom of the Forest of Bowland which was still in use as recently as 1937. Being the only courtroom between York and Lancaster, it was used by visiting Justices from the 14th century onwards and is said to have been used by Oliver Cromwell when he was in the area. The records still remain in the archives at Clitheroe Castle as well as the county archives at Preston.

Slaidburn makes a relaxing holiday retreat, and for self-catering enthusiasts Sheila Parker of **Horns Farm** has two comfortable stone-built cottages in the centre of the village which make an ideal touring base. Each is simply furnished with all the usual facilities, one sleeping 4/5 and the other sleeping 2. Both have steps leading up into a lovely rear garden which offers panoramic countryside views, but Sheila regrets, no pets are allowed. Slaidburn is a pretty village with narrow cobbled streets and the village green bordered by the River Hodder, but there are many other equally delightful places within easy reach from here, such as the Ribble Valley, the Yorkshire Dales and the Lake District.

Horns Farm, Church Street, Slaidburn Tel: 0200 446288

Slaidburn is a good centre for country walks. A network of beautiful, little visited lanes, hardly wide enough for a small car, radiate westwards into the high fell country, or eastwards into the main Ribble Valley to the charming village of Bolton-by-Bowland.

If you venture along the B6478 you will soon reach **Tosside**, a small hamlet on the edge of the Forest of Bowland, half in Lancashire and half in Yorkshire. Just over into Yorkshire is the delightfully named village of Wigglesworth.

The Plough Inn was originally a farmhouse built around 1700 and is now a pub, owned and personally run by the Goodalls, whose many years of experience in the licensing trade is immediately apparent. Well renowned for their excellent cuisine, you can choose to eat in the cosy, beamed intimacy of one restaurant situated within the main building, or alternatively opt for the conservatory restaurant which overlooks the lovely garden complete with pond and floodlit fountain. Either way, your gastronomic desires are sure to be satiated and if you haven't time to linger, there are various traditional bar meals available. Having enjoyed your meal, what could be nicer than retiring to one of the beautifully furnished, en-suite guest rooms.

The Plough Inn, Wigglesworth, Skipton Tel: 0729 840243

Carrying straight along the B6478 will bring you to the A65 road to Kendal. Turning north it will bring you to **Clapham**. It is worthwhile pausing your journey in Clapham village where there is a car park and National Park Information Centre enabling you to leave your car and follow the Nature Trail walk which leads to Clapham's **Ingleborough Cave**, the outlet cave of the famous Gaping Gill system. It contains some impressive cave formations, underground streams and naturally formed passages, with magnificent displays of cave coral and illuminated pools, all providing a unique underground experience.

Built in 1820 and originally the vicarage for the pretty village of Clapham, **Arbutus House** is the splendid home of Michael and Christine Cass who offer a warm, family welcome to all their guests. Enjoying a delightful riverside setting, this spacious guest house is attractively furnished throughout, with open fires, antique furniture and extra little touches like dishes of pot pourri all enhancing a cosy, relaxed ambience. There are six lovely guest rooms, all well equipped and most with en-suite facilities. Dining is a treat, with homecooked evening meals prepared from fresh local produce and cooked on the Aga. Special diets are readily catered for and the substantial breakfast served each morning would satisfy the heartiest appetite.

Arbutus House, Riverside, Clapham Tel: 0524 251240

Travelling west from Clapham along the B6480, you will pass through **High** and **Low Bentham**. Evidence of the antiquity of these quaint villages abounds. Near West End Farm in Low Bentham you can see remains of a Roman road which ran from Ribchester to Burrow and Castleton. In the Parish Church of St. John the Baptist there is a fragment of a crucifix, apparently of Saxon origin, thus at least a thousand years old, and the church itself receives mention in the Domesday Book, although nothing of the original building remains, it having been destroyed in the 14th century by the marauding Scots. A "Plague Stone" between High and Low Bentham is a grim reminder of the pestilence of 1597 and 1598 which played havoc with the district.

Stonegate House Restaurant, Low Bentham, Via Lancaster
Tel: 05242 61362

Both villages are ideally situated as a touring base for the Dales and The Lake District and in Low Bentham you will find **Stonegate House Restaurant**. Believed to be the oldest building in the village, it dates back to the 1600's and traditional 'cottage' style furnishings throughout enhancing an atmosphere of olde worlde charm. From the restaurant patio doors you can view the acre of beautiful gardens and dining is a gastronomic delight, with a varied and regularly changing menu offering dishes to tempt every palate. Entertainment is provided by an amazing collection of musical porcelain figurines offering a taste of nostalgia with a selection of bygone melodies. After dinner, you can put the perfect end to your evening by staying in one of the three superb en-suite guest rooms, two of which boast four poster beds.

Nearby is the village of **Higher Tatham,** where if you enjoy self-catering, you will find an idyllic holiday haven at **Ashleys Farm.** Here an attractive courtyard development from 18th century stone farmbuildings has created a small hamlet of five cottages sleeping between 2 and 6, each equipped with every modern amenity to ensure a relaxing holiday. Its location provides panoramic views towards the hills of the Yorkshire Dales and the shops, pubs and restaurants of Low and High Bentham are only a few minutes drive away. This is another of Elizabeth Parkinson's Red Rose Cottages - please telephone 0200 27310 for a brochure.

Ashleys Farm, Higher Tatham, Near Lancaster Tel: 0200 27310

Continuing southwards following the beautiful Lune Valley you can trace a picturesque route along quiet roads via Wray and Claughton, perhaps taking in Caton, which has the remains of an ancient cross, and its twin village Brookhouse.

From here we travel to the northern end of the Lune Valley and the town of Kirkby Lonsdale, which is where we begin the next chapter.

CHAPTER FOUR
North Lancashire and Lancaster

Hornby Castle

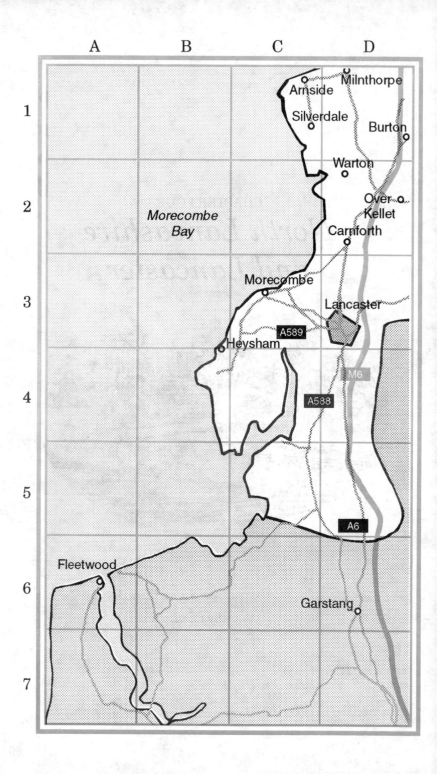

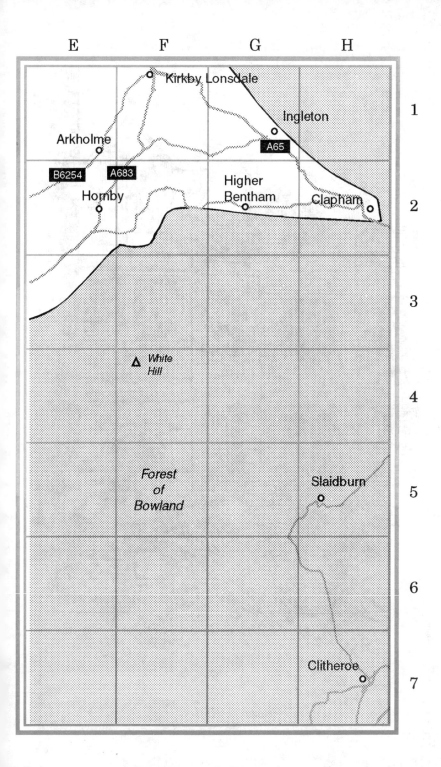

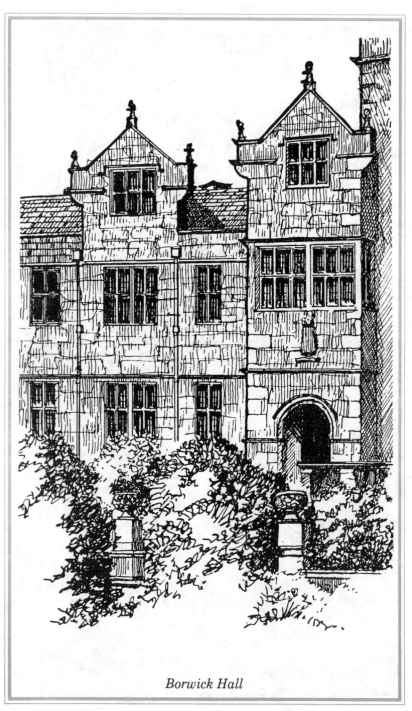

Borwick Hall

CHAPTER FOUR

North Lancashire and Lancaster

The northern edge of Lancashire sweeps from Morecambe Bay up along the valley of the River Lune to the edge of the Yorkshire Dales.

Indeed, high up on Leck Fell east of Kirkby Lonsdale, you are in true Dales country, with a typical craggy limestone gorge along the little valley of Leck Beck, as well as one of the most extensive cave systems in the British Isles for the experienced potholer to explore. We shall begin this chapter in the delightful village of **Ingleton**, over the county border, in North Yorkshire.

Here you can discover Ingleton Waterfalls, one of the noted natural Beauty Spots of the North. The Falls Walk is a spectacular four mile stretch leading up the glen, over the hills and returning down the other glen to Ingleton. The First Pecca Falls and Pecca Twin Falls are a delight to behold, as is Hollybush Spout. Thornton Force, the Triple Spout of Beezley and the Rival Falls are equally impressive, with individual splendour and beauty, and from here the rushing waters plunge and roar through Baxenghyll Gorge and over Snow Falls before returning to the village.

Riverside Lodge, Main Street, Ingleton Tel: 05242 41359

Enjoying a peaceful location in the heart of the village of Ingleton, with the River Greta running past the bottom of the garden, **Riverside Lodge** makes an idyllic holiday base. Awarded a Three Crowns Commended grading, the property has been extensively refurbished by its owners, David and Pauline Morris, and provides excellent accommodation in six beautifully furnished en-suite guest rooms within the main house as well as the two-bedroomed Coach Block with private sitting room, which can be used by self-catering guests. Dining here is a treat, with evening meals superbly cooked by David and enjoyed in candlelight in the new conservatory, with a fine accompanying wine selection. With fishing rights available and a wealth of beautiful countryside to explore, not to mention a sauna to relax in upon your return, Riverside Lodge is a super place to stay.

Kirkby Lonsdale is actually just over the Lancashire border in the county of Cumbria, but it serves as a focal point for the whole of this part of the dale. Architecturally, this little town is a jewel, with a considerable number of fine Georgian, Regency and early Victorian houses and shops.

As you approach the town along the main A65 from the east, your first sight of the town is across **Devil's Bridge**, a slender, triple-arched bridge across a wooded gorge of the River Lune. Records show this bridge being in existence as far back as 1365 when a grant of pontage - the ability to collect a toll from travellers crossing the bridge - was granted to the vicar, who in return had to maintain it. The bridge apparently takes its name from a legend about the Devil and an old lady who wanted to get her cattle to the other side of the river. The Devil promised her a bridge provided he could have the soul of the first creature to cross it. Next morning, the Devil lay in waiting for his victim, but was thwarted by the ingenuity of the old lady, who before crossing herself, threw a bun across the bridge. Her little dog chased it across and the Devil had to be content with the animal's soul instead.

Kirkby Lonsdale is a delightful little market town growing up on an old packhorse route, and during the 18th century an annual hiring fair was held there. It has a fine Market Square (market day is Thursday) with a tall Market Cross, and the attractive narrow streets radiating from the Square are lined with shops, cafés and public houses.

Take some time to admire the views - the town is wonderfully situated on a high bank overlooking the River Lune. The glorious views from the Churchyard and Ruskin's View up the valley to the Howgills and Casterton Fells have drawn many artists, including JMW Turner, and were described as "one of the loveliest scenes in England" by John Ruskin.

74

NORTH LANCASHIRE AND LANCASTER

A natural route from Kirkby Lonsdale to the county town of Lancaster is marked by the River Lune. For those who enjoy walking, the best way to enjoy this area of Lancashire is to follow the Lune Valley Ramble. The booklet that accompanys the walk (available from Kirkby Lonsdale Tourist Information Centre) provides detailed maps and plenty of information on the places which you pass. The Lune Valley Ramble allows you to explore the valley's intimate pastoral setting, with walking through woodland, meadows and along the riverside itself. You can also enjoy picturesque villages, castles and ancient churches along the way. The booklet is designed to be followed from Lancaster to Kirkby Lonsdale, however the maps are detailed enough for the route to be followed easily in either direction.

There is a lovely network of quiet lanes and roads leading out of this green and sheltered valley to delightful villages such as Whittington, Wennington, Melling, Tunstall, Wray and Gressingham, all of which repay exploration handsomely.

Tobilane Designs, Newton Holme Farm, Whittington
Tel: 05242 72662

On the B6254 Carnforth road, midway between **Whittington** and Arkholme, you will find **Newton Holme Farm**, home of Tobilane Designs, a super toy workshop where you can see traditional toys manufactured in the time-honoured way. Each item is beautifully handcrafted, from the brightly coloured wooden mobiles and intriguing Jacob's Ladder, to the wonderful ride-on Thomas the Tank Engine and woolly rocking sheep - after all why should horses have all the fun! This really is a treasure trove of delight and the only difficulty with your visit here is how to get everyone to leave - and we don't just mean the children!

On the other side of the Lune Valley, south of Kirkby Lonsdale on A683, you will find the bustling town of **Hornby**. Hornby has many

75

historic connections. Its position by a bluff overlooking the valley commands a fine panoramic view of the Lune Valley and this strategic position has been utilised over the centuries for defence purposes. Just to the north of Hornby is the attractive stone built Loyn Bridge. The bridge takes the road over the Lune to Gressingham and was built in 1684 replacing a ford. Situated beside the bridge is the Castle Stede which presents the best example of a Norman motte and bailey castle in Lancashire, built at a point which clearly controls the crossing of the Lune.

The romantically situated **Hornby Castle**, which can be viewed from the village, was immortalised in a painting by Turner, although it was only built last century, incorporating the ruins of an older castle, and transformed into a grand and picturesque country house.

In the centre of town on Main Street you will find **The Castle Hotel**. Run by Stanford and Rosalynd Robinson for the past twelve years, this charming hotel was formerly a coaching inn providing rest and refreshment for travellers between Lancaster and Kendal. The old stables and smithy are still in existence to the rear of the premises.

The Castle Hotel, Main Street, Hornby, Lancashire Tel: 0524 21204

A warm and friendly atmosphere greets the visitor to this comfortable establishment. There are twelve guest rooms, eight of which are en-suite. Two of the rooms are on the ground floor and are suitable for disabled persons. The cosy bar lounge has open log fires and Mrs. Robinson includes her own specialities in the two restaurants, making the best use of local produce. The hotel also provides morning coffee and afternoon tea and bar meals are available at lunchtime and in the evening. A beer garden offers an attractive setting for drinks outside on a warm summer's day; the distinctive 'real ale' is brewed locally at Lancaster.

The Robinsons are happy to organise river fishing and pony

76

trekking for their guests and there are squash courts and four golf courses within easy reach, as well as many places of interest.

Continuing south on the A683, shortly before entering the village of **Claughton** (pronounced Clafton) look out for the Old Toll House Garage where early this century the garage owner painted the first white lines on the road at the nearby corner because of the many accidents there. After much debate their value was recognised by King George V and from then the use of white lines became accepted, eventually spreading worldwide.

Continuing on this road just before you reach the M6 take the road to the right signed to Halton, which soon crosses the lovely stone Crook O'Line bridge. A little way over the bridge on the right there is a car park where you can leave the car and take a short stroll along the Caton footpath, created from the old Lancaster-Wennington rail line. From the old rail bridges magnificent views of the Lune and wooded banks can be enjoyed on this part of the river known as the Crook O'Lune. Gray and Turner have both acknowledged the delight of the scene.

Eventually you come to the ancient city of **Lancaster** on the River Lune. The capital of this beautiful county, it proudly boasts of its 'Legacy', which extends back many centuries. Unlike York, which has long been internationally known as a tourist attraction, its Red Rose cousin has taken longer to be discovered.

In fact, Lancaster has an equally important place in English history and there is much for the serious visitor to explore. It's also a surprisingly compact city, easily reached by either road, just off the M6, or by rail from a centrally positioned station where most Intercity trains call.

Within yards of the railway station you'll find **Lancaster Castle**, a great medieval fortress, founded by Normans to keep out Scottish invaders, and strengthened by John of Gaunt, Duke of Lancaster, in the 15th century. Standing proudly atop a hill, this great medieval castle has an imposing presence and dominates the skyline above Lancaster. Its huge square keep dates back to 1200 and was raised in height and impregnability at the time of The Armada. Astonishingly perhaps, most of the building still functions as a prison, but certain sections are open to the public, including the 18th century Shire Hall, the cells, where the witches of Pendle were imprisoned, the Crown Court, Hadrian's Tower and, a touch of the macabre, the Drop Room where prisoners were prepared for the gallows.

Close by, sharing the hill with the Castle, is a building with less grim associations - the lovely **Priory Church of St. Mary**, which once served a Benedictine Priory established here in 1094. Most of the present church dates from the 14th and 15th centuries, and particularly interesting things to see are fragments of Anglo-Saxon crosses, magnificent medieval choir stalls, and some very fine needlework. Nearby is a link with Roman Lancaster - the remains of a bath house which also served soldiers as an inn.

A short walk from the Castle leads into the largely pedestrianised city centre, for shops, the market and much besides. **The City Museum** in the Market Place occupies the Old Town Hall, built between 1781-3 by Major Jarrett and Thomas Harrison. As well as the city's art collection and an area of changing exhibitions, you'll find displays and collections of material illustrating aspects of the city's industrial and social history. Also here is the **Museum of the King's Own Royal Regiment**, a regiment which was based in Lancaster from 1880 onwards.

J. Atkinson & Co., China Street, Lancaster Tel: 0524 65470

As you walk into **J. Atkinson & Co**. on China Street, you can be forgiven for feeling you have slipped into a timewarp, for this delightful tea and coffee merchant's is exactly as it has been for generations, with assistants in brown overalls, old machinery and even the original tins on the shelves bearing the Lancaster City coat of arms, all adding an air of bygone days. Established in 1837, the year that Queen Victoria came to the throne, this wonderful shop specialises in coffee which they roast on the premises daily and a glorious aroma hits you the minute you walk in. Among the many people they supply is the Sunbury Coffee House.

In Church Street is the **Judges Lodging**, a beautifully proportioned building dating from the 1620s when it was built as a private house for Thomas Covell, but later used for judges during the Lancaster Assizes. It now houses two separate museums; the **Museum of Childhood** containing the Barry Elder doll collection, and a **Fur-**
78

Judges Lodging, Lancaster

Heysham Church

niture Museum containing many examples of the workmanship of Gillows, the famous Lancaster cabinet makers. In fact it was Richard Gillow who designed the Maritime Museum.

Around the corner in Sun Street is the **Music Room**, an exquisite early Georgian building originally designed as a pavilion in the long vanished garden of Oliver Marton. It is notable for some superb decorative plasterwork.

Tucked away close by in Music Room Square, is a little gem called **Sunbury Coffee House**. The Georgian theme extends from the attractive stone facade to the elegant interior with its marble table tops and this provides the perfect setting in which to enjoy the finest selection of tea and coffee accompanied by delicious freshly prepared snacks. Ranging from jacket potatoes with a choice of fillings to open sandwiches and savoury filled croissants, not to mention a mouth-watering display of homemade cakes and pastries, Sunbury Coffee House is a very tempting stopping-off point as you explore the wonders of this historic city.

Sunbury Coffee House, Music Room Square, 28 Sun Street,
Lancaster Tel: 0524 843312

Lancaster has grown up by the River Lune, navigable as far as Skerton Bridge, so there has always been a strong association between the town and its watery highway. It was in the late 17th and 18th centuries that Lancaster's character as a port fully emerged. The splendid buildings of the 18th century 'Golden Age' were born out of the port wealth, and the layout and appearance of the town was much altered by this building bonanza. Lancaster as a port gradually declined throughout the 19th century so that many buildings put up for specific maritime purposes were taken over for other uses. Naturally the city has been affected by the arrival of the canal, the railways and 19th century industry; yet the hallmark of Lancaster, its Georgian centre, remains as the product of this maritime prosperity.

Lancaster's rich maritime history is celebrated at St. George's Quay, which with its great stone warehouses and superb Custom House, is now an award-winning **Maritime Museum**. In Georgian times this was a thriving port with the warehouses receiving ship-loads of mahogany, tobacco, rum and sugar from the West Indies. Visitors today are given a vivid insight into the life of the mariners and quayside workers, with opportunities for Knot tying and other mari-time skills. Every year, over the four days of Easter weekend, St. George's Quay is the site home to the Lancaster Maritime Festival with Smugglers, Sea Songs and Shanties. If you're in the area, or even if you're not, it's well worth a visit.

For a peaceful and relaxing afternoon, a canalboat trip is ideal, providing a leisurely way to explore some of most beautiful stretches of countryside. At **Penny Street Bridge Wharf** in the city centre, you can join public canal cruises which travel over the Lune Aqueduct, the finest stone aqueduct in the country, built in 1797 by famous engineer John Rennie. The trips last an hour and a half and re-freshments are available on this magnificent 60 foot narrow boat. If you prefer to travel under your own steam, you can hire a punt by the hour or the day or follow the meandering towpath by mountain bike (also available for hire).

Penny Street Bridge Wharf, Lancaster
Tel: 0524 849484 or 0836 633189

Built between 1797 and 1819, the **Lancaster Canal** stretches 57 miles from Preston through the centre of Lancaster to Kendal. Today it is navigable between Preston and Tewitfield, north of Lancaster, the longest lock-free stretch of canal in the country. The canal offers a diversity of scenery and wildlife with opportunities for long distance trips and short circular walks with fine views through peaceful countryside. With 41 lock-free miles it offers relaxed boating with canalside pubs, restaurants and boat-hire facilities. It provides a good touring route for canoeists and is excellent for coarse fishing.

Another place the whole family can enjoy is Lancaster Leisure Park on Wyresdale Road. Set in 42 acres of landscaped parkland, the site includes a mini-marina, a Wild West adventure playground, miniature railway, rare breeds unit, children's farmyard, pony rides, gift shop, tea garden and pottery shop.

While exploring the city it is worth travelling via East Road and Wyresdale Road on the eastern edge, to Williamson Park. Here you can see the impressive **Ashton Memorial** - a great green copper-domed building, a kind of miniature St. Paul's - standing on a hilltop

The Old Bath House, Sunderland Point

in the centre of a wonderful Edwardian park. It forms a landmark seen for miles around and gives a magnificent viewpoint across Morecambe Bay, the Lakeland Hills and the Forest of Bowland. It now houses exhibitions and multi-screen presentations about the Life and Times of Lancaster's Lord Ashton and The Edwardians. There is also a delightful Tropical Butterfly House in the former conservatory.

Featuring prominently on the Lancashire coastline, **Morecambe** has long been one of the most successful and popular seaside resorts in the North, and it can truly be said to enjoy one of the finest views from its promenade of any resort in England - a magnificent sweep of coastline and bay, looking across to the Lakeland mountains. Like other resorts, Morecambe has changed with the times, and major new attractions include the multi-million pound Bubbles Leisure Park and Superdome, as well as a Wild West Theme Park. WOMAD, Morecambe's annual world music festival, attracts visitors from across the globe. There are also popular seafront Illuminations in late summer, together with all the usual lively shops and variety of entertainment associated with a busy seaside resort.

It's worth strolling along the promenade as far as **Heysham**, Morecambe's twin, with its quaint old main street which winds down to the shore. It is also a town with considerable historic associations, because it was here in the 8th century that Christian missionaries arrived from Ireland to convert the heathen Viking settlers in the north of England. They built the chapel of St. Patrick on a rock on the sea edge. Its ruins, with coffin-shaped rocks - one of the most curious graveyards in England - can still be seen.

The little church of St. Peter's on the headland is equally interesting. It dates back to Saxon and Norman times, with an Anglo-Saxon cross on which the Madonna and other figures have been crudely carved by 9th century masons, and there is a rare Viking hog-back gravestone.

Alongside these antiquities is the modern port of Heysham, with regular car-ferry sailings to the Isle of Man and to Northern Ireland.

For anyone with a sense of the past, it is worth making your way further down the peninsula formed by Heysham and the River Lune, via Middleton and Overton, from where you can either walk or drive (though be careful - the road is closed at high tide, and parking is extremely limited in the village) to **Sunderland Point**. This is, unbelievably, an old port and seaside resort, which flourished until larger berthed ships, silting channels and the growth last century of rail-served Morecambe caused it to decline. A little wharf, quiet cottages, some with faded and evocative elegance, a sandy shore where sea thrift flourishes among the pebbles, are all that remains.

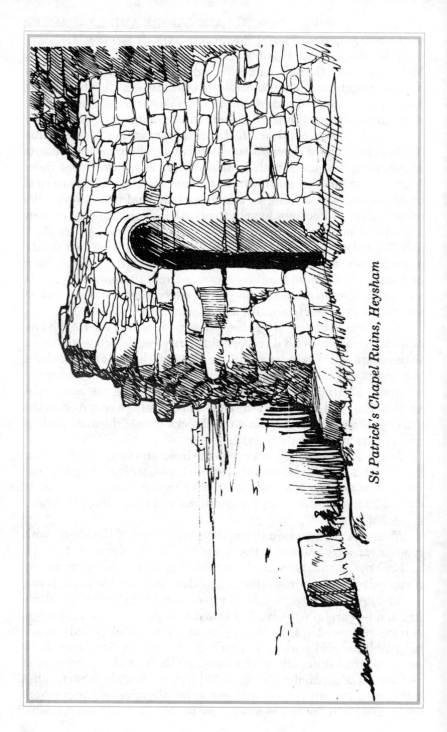

St Patrick's Chapel Ruins, Heysham

The estuary is now a Site of Special Scientific Interest because of its wildlife value. You are likely to see such birds as redshank feeding on the rich food supplies of worms, shellfish and shrimps on the saltmarshes, while a variety of wildfowl such as shelduck, wigeon and mallard, are to be seen in autumn.

A particularly sad story is associated at Sunderland with Sambo's grave, Sambo was a sea captain's servant at the time of the Slave Trade into Lancaster, who probably died of a fever in 1736 after a long and difficult voyage from the West Indies. Because he was not a baptised Christian, he was not allowed to be buried in consecrated ground. In later years, his death and grave became a potent local symbol of the anti-slavery cause.

His grave can be still seen, in a field at the west side of the point. It is reached by walking along The Lane from the village foreshore, past Upsteps Cottage where Sambo died, and turning left at the shore then over a stile on the left which gives access to the simple grave-stone. Fresh flowers are usually to be seen here, mysteriously placed on the grave.

On the opposite side of the Lune estuary from Sunderland Point (and only reached by a long road journey through Lancaster) is **Glasson Dock**. The silting of the Lune that ended Lancaster's importance as a port was the reason for the building of Glasson Dock in 1787 to hold 25 seagoing ships. In 1825, the Lancaster Canal was built to provide a better link between the city and the docks, and this was, in turn, supplemented by a railway line in 1883. This railway is now the footpath and cycle way to Lancaster's St. George's Quay.

Thurnham Mill Hotel, Conder Green, Near Thurnham, Lancashire
Tel: 0524 752852

However, the village of Glasson is now a sailing centre, with the old canal basin a popular marina, and the old wharves and warehouses

85

transformed into an attractive leisure area, with pubs and shops serving a different kind of sea-going clientele.

You can walk, cycle or drive from Glasson past Plover Scar where a lighthouse guards the estuary, and where you'll find, near the point where the little River Cocker flows into the Lune, the ruins of **Cockersand Abbey**. The Abbey was founded in 1190 by the Premonstratensian Order on the site of a hospital. This had been the abode of a hermit, Hugh Garth, before becoming a colony for lepers and the infirm. The Chapter House of the Abbey remains, and was a burial chapel for the Daltons of Thurnham, descendants of Sir Thomas Moore.

A little way from here, just off the A588, lies the village of **Thurnham**. If you are looking for somewhere a little different as a holiday base, or just seeking good food in pleasant surroundings, then at **Thurnham Mill Hotel** you won't be disappointed. This Four Crown Commended establishment enjoys a lovely canalside location close to Lancaster Golf Club. Originally a 19th century corn mill, sympathetic conversion in 1991 has preserved the building's unique character whilst providing every modern amenity. Huge beams and original flagstone floors together with traditional furnishings enhance the olde worlde ambience which extends into the eighteen en-suite guest rooms. You can relax with a drink on the canalside terrace and the restaurant which is open to non-residents offers a superb menu combined with friendly efficient service. All these factors make Thurnham Mill a popular venue with locals and tourists alike.

Whitewalls Restaurant, Hatlex Lane, Hest Bank, Lancaster Tel:
0524 822768

Venturing north from Morecambe you will come to the quiet village of **Hest Bank** where, tucked away up Hatlex Lane between the village and the A6 road to Carnforth, you will discover **Whitewalls Res-**

taurant - another 'hidden' gem well worth seeking out. With ready access for disabled visitors, this superb restaurant is set within a listed building once the home of local character William Stout, a Lancashire shopkeeper. The surroundings are sumptuous without being impersonal, with many extra little touches which ensure that it provides the perfect setting in which to savour an extensive and imaginative à la carte menu plus a range of daily specials which incorporate the finest English and Continental cuisine. It comes as no surprise therefore to learn that Whitewalls has won the Best Kept Restaurant award several times, a factor which makes eating here such a joy.

To the north of Lancaster, the town of **Carnforth** lies around what used to be a busy crossroads on the A6. It has a choice of inns and shops, including one of the largest bookshops (new and secondhand) in Lancashire.

Carnforth was once a busy railway junction town whose station has a claim to fame as the setting for the 1940s film classic 'Brief Encounter'. Though the station has declined in importance, being an unstaffed halt, the old engine sheds and sidings are now occupied by **Steamtown**, one of the largest steam railway centres in the north of England. You are likely to see such giants of the Age of Steam as the Flying Scotsman or an A4 Pacific being stabled here, together with a permanent collection of over 30 British and Continental steam locomotives. There are steam rides in the summer months on both standard gauge and miniature lines.

The Lodge, Netherbeck, Carnforth Tel: 0200 27310

Just a mile from Carnforth, on a quiet holiday home park at Netherbeck, you will find a lovely place to stay at **The Lodge**, a distinctly upmarket pine-built lodge which carries a Four Keys Highly Commended rating. Furnished and equipped to a very high

Carnforth Steam Railway

standard, The Lodge has all you need to ensure a totally relaxing holiday and enjoys a peaceful location with views across open farmland towards Warton Crag. Lying at the gateway to the Lake District, it makes an ideal touring base from which to explore the surrounding countryside. Managed by Red Rose Cottages - telephone 0200 27310 for a brochure.

In the most northern part of Lancashire is Morecambe Bay and the Kent estuary. The villages of **Silverdale** and **Arnside** (actually in Cumbria) are small and mainly residential, but are worth visiting for the network of footpaths crossing the escarpments whose limestone woodlands are a joy for the botanist, being rich in wild flowers in spring - primroses, violets, orchids, bird's eye primroses, rockroses and eglantines abound. You can take a choice of footpaths from Arnside village to the summit of the lovely little limestone hill called Arnside Knott, to enjoy breathtaking views of the Kent Estuary, and across Morecambe Bay. Another footpath follows the shoreline around the little peninsula, following a miniature cliff above the muddy estuary which is particularly rich in birdlife - both seabirds and a variety of waders. If you continue inland by quiet lanes or footpaths you will soon reach **Arnside Tower**, a 14th century pele tower, built during the reign of Edward II.

Beetham, on the A6 further inland, has an unusual 19th century Post Office with a distinctive black-and-white studded door. Within earshot of a waterfall is the **Church of St Michael and All angels**, approached through a pergola of rambling roses. The church dates from Saxon times and during restoration work in 1834, a hoard of about one hundred old coins was discovered. The coins were from the reigns of Edward the Confessor, William the Conqueror and William Rufus. In the Civil War the church was badly damaged, its windows smashed and effigies broken. However, a glass fragment of Henry IV in an ermine robe has survived.

Heron Corn Mill, nearby, is a restored and working water-mill, with fully operational grinding machinery. There is an exhibition about its history and the processes of milling. Just outside the village, on the Arnside road, a sign points the way to Fairy Steps, a curious rock formation in the woods.

Leighton Moss near Silverdale is a nationally known RSPB Bird Sanctuary, while bird lovers will also enjoy a visit to nearby **Leighton Hall**. As well as being a handsome neo-Gothic building with exceptional collections of Lancaster-made Gillow furniture, the Hall has extensive grounds which are used for displays of falconry in the summer months.

From here we turn southwards and make our way to the lovely districts of Fylde and Wyre and thus into the next chapter.

Arnside Tower

CHAPTER FIVE

The Fylde and Wyre

Croston Village

91

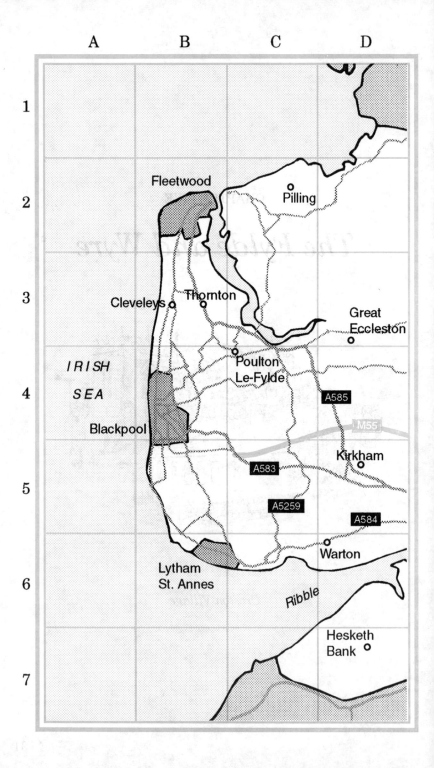

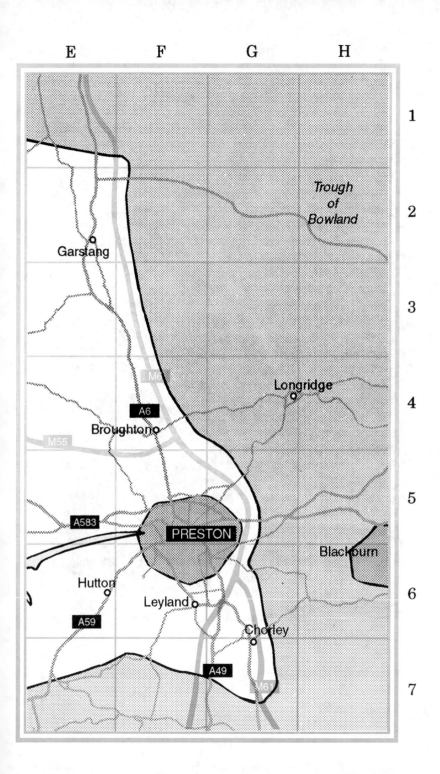

Lytham Hall

The Fylde and Wyre

South of Lancaster just off the A6 lies **Garstang**, an ancient, picturesque town whose market dates back to the time of King Edward II, who gave monks the right to hold a market here. It was also important as a stage coaching town on the great high road to Scotland, and Bonnie Prince Charlie is reputed to have stayed in the town in 1715. The main road, later the A6, now by-passes the town, as does the M6. Garstang also had a period of glory as an inland port on the Lancaster Canal and there are a number of fine canalside features, and trip boats operate on the canal during the summer time.

On Thursdays, the weekly market takes over the town, and the High Street and Market Hall become a hive of activity.

About half a mile east of the town on a grassy knoll are the ruins of **Greenhaigh Castle**, built in 1490 by Thomas Stanley, the first Earl of Derby. The castle was severely damaged in a siege against Cromwell in 1645-46, reputedly one of the last strongholds in Lancashire to hold out against him.

A little to the north on the A6 look out for the remains of a stone built toll house, probably dating from the 1820's when parts of the turnpike from Garstang to Lancaster and beyond were re-aligned - the old road snakes from side to side of the present A6. More than usually interesting because the posts for the toll gate still exist on either side of the road.

When driving through the area try and keep an eye out for the Garstang Milestones. They are to be seen to the North and South of Garstang on the A6, and are the finest turnpike milestones in the County. To the south, they are round-faced stones with cursive lettering dating from the 1750's. To the north the stones are triangular, with Roman lettering associated with the realignments of the 1820's.

Garstang has an excellent **Discovery Centre** in the High Street, which deals with a variety of aspects of the region, including the canal and countryside history, both in Over Wyre and the nearby Forest of Bowland.

South of Garstang there are some attractive villages to explore. **Churchtown**, for example, is a delightful village with many build-

Greenhalgh Castle, Garstang

ings of architectural and historical interest. The church of St. Helens dates back to the Norman Conquest and includes architecture from almost every period since then. There is a museum of dolls and toys from the last 100 years at the local school. Find out much more about Churchtown - pick up a village trail leaflet from the church.

Next to the parish church of St. Helen in the centre of the village stands the award-winning **Punchbowl Inn and Restaurant**. This really is a first class hostelry, from its attractive black and white exterior which entices you inside, to the lovely character bar, with its exposed oak beams and open log fires enhancing the warm, friendly atmosphere. A former 16th century coaching inn, The Punchbowl is renowned for its excellent food, and welcoming hosts David and Pat Singleton have won the Huntsman Awards prestigious title 'Licensee of the Year'. In the cosy surroundings of the three bars you can enjoy a pint of fine hand-pulled ale and to the rear of the pub, the lovely restaurant provides a relaxing setting for an excellent homecooked meal. Families are most welcome and smaller portions are available for children and those with smaller appetites.

The Punchbowl Inn, Church Street, Churchtown, Garstang Tel: 0995 603360

Idyllic - that is the only description that can be applied to **Guy's Thatched Hamlet** - the something for everyone spot. Neatly tucked away by the side of the Lanacaster canal, off the main A6 road at **Bilsborrow**, near Garstang, it is on the fringe of an extensive motorway network taking in the M6, M61 and M55.

This is a family-run business provides a variety of services, set in a cosy, hamlet style farmhouse, dating back to the 15th century. The restaurant, Guy's Eating Establishment, is tastefully informal and among other delights, serves excellent Italian food. Guests can watch the chefs spinning and throwing the dough to make the pizza bases.

97

'Owd Nell's, is a flagged floored thatched countrystyle tavern, and is renowned for it's range of cask kept ales, wine and lagers from across the world. It is named after 'Owd Nell, a local character from the early 18th century who ran her barge on the nearby canal, carrying coal. Food is also served in the tavern and the menu includes dishes such as a tankard of un-shelled prawns, fish, chips and mushy peas and our famous home-made steak and kidney puddings, among other traditional bar favourites. The School House Square nearby, is home to 'Owd Nell's craft shops, the ice cream parlour and a kiddies play area.

Accommodation is available at Guy' Lodgings, a recent addition, but thatched and in keeping with the hamlet. You can always drive in when you need a room, but it is a good idea to book ahead. Reservations on 0995 640849.

Guy's Thatched Hamlet, St. Michaels Road, Bilsborrow,
near Garstang, Preston Tel: 0995 640010/640020

Crossing to the other side of the M6 you will find yourself on the edge of the Forest of Bowland, area of natural beauty. This western area of Bowland lies within a network of quiet lanes, with hidden villages such as Claughton, Calder Vale and Oakenclough. From the higher lanes along the moorland edges, you get sudden, unexpected views of the Fylde Coast, and often magnificent sunsets looking across the Irish Sea. Best of all, this is an area to explore on foot. Leaving the car and the tarmac roads, you can take a choice of footpaths, for example, winding along the little River Brock, or onto the higher fell country around Bleasdale.

In the village of **Claughton**, lovers of fine clothes will discover a real haven at Country Vogue. Attractively restored stables, once the home of prizewinning Shire horses, now house a vast collection of quality country clothing, ranging from designer labels to wax jackets, handbags and accessories. You can choose from a selection of classic

98

pure wool knitwear, all cotton shirts, handcrafted leather shoes and other beautiful items made from the finest yarn and cloth, be it alpaca, silk or cashmere and all of which look quite at home in rooms where flagstoned floors and beamed ceilings retain the original character of these old buildings.

Country Vogue, Garstang Road, Claughton-on-Brock, Garstang Tel: 0995 640622

Just a little to the east is **Beacon Fell Country Park**, one of the most popular countryside destinations in this part of Lancashire. This is a beautiful wooded hill top, commanding magnificent views of the Bowland Fells. There are well-signed car parks, picnic places and a choice of well-marked walks across the summit and through the woodlands, and the area is rich in wildlife interest.

Returning to the other side of the M6, continue west on the A586 towards Poulton. A few miles beyond Churchtown is the village of St. Michael's-on-Wyre. It has a superb church, mainly 15th century, but with Jacobean pews and some unusual stained glass.

Continuing on this road, deviate only slightly to stop off at the village of **Great Eccleston** which lies in the centre of the Fylde plain, 10 miles from Blackpool and 12 miles from Preston. Every Wednesday the busy Open Air Market held in the picturesque Village Square attracts local villagers, residents from neighbouring villages and even coach parties from outside the rural area. The parish council began negotiations to have a market in 1971, and by 1974 they were successful. Some 20 - 30 stalls sell a variety of goods and are open for business from 10am to 4pm.

In Great Eccleston, at West End, you will discover a real gem of a restaurant called **Ferrari's**. Now a Grade II listed building, it boasts carefully preserved cruck beams and at the front of the restaurant the original mud wall lies exposed under glass for all to see. This

99

delightful restaurant is run by Gino and Susan Ferrari and their family and, not surprisingly, the 'Ferrari' theme extends from the decor to the menu, with a range of individual steak dishes named after this prestigious Italian car. For example, should you choose a Ferrari F40, you will be served with a delicious fillet steak covered with a mouthwatering prawn sauce. A warm, friendly atmosphere pervades throughout and Susan's culinary expertise is complemented by Gino's excellent front of house service. This is definitely a place where you can sample Ferrari quality at low prices - don't miss it!

Ferrari's Restaurant, West End, Great Eccleston Tel: 0995 70243

Not far from Poulton-le-Fylde, and situated on the B5260 is the village of **Singleton**. Here you will find the Millers Arms.

The Millers Arms, Weeton Road, Singleton Tel: 0253 882668

Part of the Beefeater chain, **The Millers Arms** is a pub and restaurant with a good reputation for its food. Recently refurbished the restaurant area has been divided into cosy alcoves formed by timber

100

beams and rustic bricks. A unique feature here is the small waterfall and bridge, between the bar and restaurant areas. The atmosphere is enhanced by the rustic decoration throughout on the miller theme and the open log fires. Good news for parents is that there is a self-contained, indoor children's play area with ball pool as well as facilities outside.

You will discover an excellent place to stay just outside Singleton. **Singleton Lodge** is a superb country house hotel recommended by the Michelin Guide and Which? Good Hotel Guide. Built in 1702 as the Manor House, it is said to have been used as a boarding school for Refined Young Ladies. Today it is an elegant hotel set in five acres of beautiful gardens and exudes a peaceful, relaxed ambience. All of the guest rooms are en-suite and individually styled, some even boasting four poster beds. Alan and Ann Smith are super hosts who go out of their way to ensure you enjoy your stay here.

Singleton Lodge, Lodge Lane, Singleton Tel: 0253 883854

Poulton-le-Fylde is a kaleidoscope of colour and old world charm. This ancient market town with its cobbled streets, market place complete with medieval stocks, and historic church makes the perfect setting for the superb floral decorations that adorn the town each year. Small wonder that Poulton has twice won the prestigious Britain in Bloom, small town category.

Poulton-le-Fylde is mentioned in the Domesday Book and once famous for its market, the town grew around the Parish Church of St. Chad's which is surrounded by several old pubs - no doubt a legacy to the days when hostelries had to cater for the thirsts of visiting farmers and market traders! Poulton's fascinating history can be traced on one of the regular Town Trails organised by the local Historical Society, details of which are available from Tourist Information Centres.

In contrast to its ancient centre, Poulton has superb 20th century

101

style shopping arcades, a modern swimming centre, and with ample free parking in the heart of the town, all amenities àre easily accessible for visitors. For the more active, Poulton has one of the Wyre's superb golf courses - a testing 9 hole course surrounded by farm and fields.

Renowed for its warmth and hospitality, this charming town with its historic buildings and friendly atmosphere, attracts visitors year after year.

It's hard to imagine the town of Poulton as a seaport today, after all, it is miles from the sea. But in bygone times, ships sailed up the Wyre to Skippool Creek, Poulton - and to Wardleys Creek across the river at Hambleton. Now Skippool is home to the Blackpool and Fleetwood Yacht Club and you can stroll by the river and see the ocean-going yachts that compete in major races around Britain.

Just off the A585, to the north of Poulton, at the roundabout by the River Wyre Hotel you will find **Little Thornton**. In a lovely spot here, by Skippool Creek is **Thornton Lodge**. This establishment has recently been refurbished, but retains its cosy character. The restaurant serves steak, fish and vegetarian meals and bar food is available in the bar areas, both serve food seven days a week. To drink you will find cask ales and regular guest beers. The garden has a patio area with benches and tables, and is ideal for sitting out on summer evenings.

Thornton Lodge, Skippool Road, Little Thornton, near Poulton Tel: 0253 882455

Heading up towards Fleetwood, you reach Thornton. They wrote about Thornton in the Domesday Book, but neighbouring Cleveleys is a child of the 20th century. Today, the blend of old and new has really put **Thornton-Cleveleys** on the map.

Thornton, on the banks of the Wyre, was a farming area and in

1794 Marsh Mill was built to grind corn. Now, the magnificent mill with its machinery restored and new sails fitted, is the centrepiece for a new development with the creation of attractive leisure facilities on land beside the mill. A visit to the speciality shops in the complex is a must. Look out for the fascinating **Northern Clog Museum**. A country park is planned for the Stanah area by the river where winding lanes and footpaths recall Thornton's old farming days.

The Blackpool-Fleetwood tramway link is unique, and it runs right through the middle of Cleveleys. Hop off at Victoria Square and you're in the heart of one of the busiest shopping areas in the Borough of Wyre, with a range of goodies on offer all along Victoria Road West.

Cleveleys seafront has long been a holiday haven with plenty of sand and lots to do. There's history here too. Cleveleys began to grow after an architectural competition was organised in 1906 and prizes were given for the best designs. Among those involved was the future Sir Edwin Lutyens, designer of modern Whitehall.

Thornton-Cleveleys has much to offer the discerning traveller - coast, countryside and more - all within easy accessible reach.

In just 160 years, **Fleetwood** has endured the transformation from wild sandhills into a busy seaport and typical Victorian resort, and now stands on the threshold of a new century with plans to further develop the new marina complex into a spectacular harbour village. Over a century and a half ago, local Squire, Sir Peter Hesketh Fleetwood hired Decimus Burton, a leading architect of the day, to draw up a grand design for the town. Plans included Queens Terrace, the spectacular North Euston Hotel - still as elegant today - a railway station to bring visitors from Northern Industrial towns, and a splendid port that was set to rival Liverpool.

Here, "where the river winds down to the sea", is a town that owes much of its prosperity to the sea. In the early days mighty ships brought in cargoes of cotton and grain from America. Gradually a new cargo took over as sailors turned their skills fishing and Fleetwood developed into the country's third largest fishing port.

Watersports are becoming increasingly popular and the town is now a major centre for the sport of sailboarding. Alternatively, you could board the popular "Steam Packet Boat" to the Isle of Man.

Look out for some of the town's more unusual features, such as the Pharos Lighthouse in the middle of the street and the unique public tramway system that runs through the heart of the town.

And of course, no self respecting British seaside resort would be complete without a pier! Fleetwood is also just the place to buy your bucket and spade and head for the beach.

For something completely different walk across the road to the

Windmill at Thornton-Cleveleys

Mount Seaside Park and stand inside the huge clock while the wheels wizz around and bells chime! This unusual building houses the Fleetwood Civic Society display and a craft centre where you can by a wide range of quality goods. The tower affords splendid views of the town and a panorama across Morecambe Bay to the Lakeland Hills.

While in the area, you will find an enjoyable trip is to take the passenger ferry across the Wyre estuary to **Knott End**. Although Knott End is little more than a hamlet, the estuary itself and the coastline are particularly interesting, with areas of mud flat, salt marsh and dunes, all rich in birdlife. Much of the area has been declared a Site of Special Scientific Interest for its unique environmental quality, and you can follow the public right of way along the coastline almost as far as Pilling, overlooking Presall Sands.

Knott End also marks one end of the Wyre Way, Fleetwood being the other. The Wyre Way is a 16 mile walk that explores the history and wildlife of the estuary and surrounding countryside, from the estuary mouth inland as far as the Shard Bridge. The route is easy to follow with clear markers - watch out for very high tides which may effect parts of the walk. For more details contact the nearest Tourist Information Centre.

A little further along the coast is **Pilling**. Pilling is a quiet scattered village on the edge of richly fertile marshland. For many years, the village was linked to its market town of Garstang by a little winding single-track railway, known affectionately to locals as the 'Pilling Pig'. Pilling is said to be the second largest village in Britain and is steeped in history. **The Olde Ship Inn**, for example, which can be found in the centre of the village, was built in 1782 by Geirge Dickson, a slave trader. Originally an inn, this listed building is reputed to be haunted by a lady dressed in Georgian attire, wandering around with a pale and worried look on her face!

The **Springfield House Hotel** in Wheel Lane, Pilling, is situated just off the A588. It is ideally positioned for business people and holidaymakers alike, as access to the M6 motorway and A6 trunk road is close by. Springfield House was built by a Yorkshire family who settled in Pilling in the early 1800's, and is a fine example of Georgian architecture. This imposing residence has been carefully looked after and nurtured by Elizabeth and Gordon Cookson, who are the resident proprietors.

Set in the peaceful surroundings of the Fylde countryside, it is only a quarter of a mile from the sea, yet conveniently placed for visits to Blackpool, Morecambe, the Lake District, and the Trough of Bowland. This four star commended hotel is beautifully furnished in keeping with its original splendour, and lends itself to sales conferences, private house parties and small exhibitions. Throughout the hotel, guests will find an abundance of fresh flowers, and most of the bedrooms have lovely four poster beds and spotlessly clean en-suite bathrooms. The restaurant is superbly appointed and caters for weekday lunches, evening meals and traditional Sunday lunches. Wedding receptions are a speciality of the house, and the beautifully manicured gardens are ideal for wedding photographs. Springfield House is more than just a hotel - it is an experience not to be missed.

Springfield House Hotel, Wheel Lane, Pilling Tel: 0253 790301

Just off the A588, heading South towards **Scronkey**, is Bradshaw Lane, where you can find **Bell Farm.**

Bell Farm, Bradshaw Lane, Scronkey, Pilling, Preston
Tel: 0253 790324

Bell Farm is an unusual establishment run by Beryl Richardson, with a Tearoom, gift shop and B&B. The Tearooms offer lunches and afternoon teas with a wide range of choice, from light snacks to steaks.

Blackpool Tower

All food is home-made, with some very fine home-baked cakes. On Sundays a traditional roast dinner is available. There are 4 bedrooms upstairs with a farmhouse feel, offered on a bed and breakfast basis. The Country Cupboard sells crafts, gifts, dried flowers, basketware and pine furniture. This part of the farm was once the bull pen.

Bell Farm is no longer a working farm but there are still animals kept here to entertain the children, and they will find horses, pigs, goats and cows. Bell Farm is open every day during the summer, except Mondays. Bed and Breakfast is available all year.

The village of **Preesall** is an ancient settlement built on a hill and one of the larger villages of Over Wyre. The name of Preesall comes from the Celtic for 'hill with brushwood growing on it'.

Rather than taking a ferry across from Fleetwood, an alternative way of crossing the Wyre is to take the A588 at Shard Bridge.

The 325 yards long **Shard Bridge** built in 1864 is on the original site of a ford across the narrow part of the River Wyre. Finds at the site certainly date it back to Roman times, and it is possible that the ford goes back even further to the Iron Age, around 500 BC. The Victorian bridge still operates a toll charge which has been paid over the decades by local residents who otherwise had to rely on the ferries or take their chances of being swept away, 'wagons and all', even at low tide!

The road shortly brings you to **Hambleton**, from where a network of quiet and sometimes extremely narrow lanes wind through a countryside of great charm. In Medieval times Hambleton was a centre for shipbuilding. A little to the north, a unique feature is the numerous Brine Wells, where brine is extracted for the chemical industry from many underground wells.

On the A588, between Hambleton and Preesall, is **Stalmine Village** where can take tea in **The Old Trough** organic tearooms situated in a traditional farmyard dominated by a superb example of a Tudor Barn.

It doesn't take long to drive south from here to **Blackpool**, probably Britain's liveliest and most popular resort. 1994 signifies a major landmark in the history of this bustling seaside town, for its world famous 518 feet high tower, copied from Paris's scarcely more famous Eiffel, celebrates its centenary and in recognition of this will be painted gold, making it an even more prominent feature!

It is hard then to believe that a little over 150 years ago, Blackpool was little more than a fishing village among sand dunes on the Irish Sea coast. In the early years, travel to and from the town involved considerable discomfort, taking two days from Yorkshire and a day from Manchester. However, the arrival of the great Victorian railway companies who laid their tracks to the coast and built their stations, of which Blackpool had three, provided cheap excursions to Blackpool for day-trippers from Lancashire and Yorkshire and so this fishing village gradually transformed into the vibrant seaside resort you find today.

The famous **Pleasure Beach** boasts its own railway station and is an attraction that continues to be extended and improved. It is now home to the tallest (235ft high), fastest (85mph), highest-tech and possibly most expensive (£12m) roller coaster ride in the world - not something to be undertaken by the fainthearted! Nearby, The Sandcastle provides all-weather fun, with waves, waterslides and flumes in a tropical indoor setting, and further down Blackpool's Golden Mile, the **Sea Life Centre** proves popular with all ages, giving visitors a close-up view of the underwater world.

Of course, the one thing that Blackpool is perhaps best renowned for is its spectacular autumn Illuminations which bring in thousands of visitors each year, all eager to witness the greatest free show on earth. As well as these modern attractions, Blackpool still retains more traditional and gentle diversions, such as tea-dances in the elegant **Tower Ballroom**.

This is all a far cry from Blackpool's first place of amusement, Uncle Tom's cabin, which perched precariously on the crumbling cliffs to the north of the town. Unfortunately the original building was lost to the sea in 1907.

The 1890s saw the development of many of the resort's now famous attractions. At that time it was estimated that Blackpool's 7,000 dwellings could accommodate 250,000 holidaymakers in addition to a permanent population of 35,000. Naturally these visitors would require entertainment and so the work began. In 1889 the original Opera House was built in the Winter Gardens complex and two years later a start was made on the "Eiffel Tower".**The North Pier** was designed by Eugenious Birch and opened on 23rd May 1963. It soon became an exclusive promenade for 'quality' visitors and is now a Listed Building.

Despite its reputation as a vibrant and lively resort, Blackpool also has its quiet corners where you can escape the hustle of crowds. You only have to walk or take a tram along a few of the seven miles of its long promenade past North Shore and Bispham, or down to Squire's Gate or Lytham St. Anne's to find life moving at a much gentler pace, with much quieter beaches and promenades, rolling dunes, and pleasant town centres, yet still enjoying the bracing sea air for which Blackpool is renowned.

There's no nicer or more enjoyable way of exploring the quieter sides of Blackpool and Wyre than by tram. The world's first electric street tramway opened in Blackpool on 29th September 1885 and ran from Cocker Street to South Shore. The route was extended along the Lytham road in 1895 and later connected with the system operated by the Blackpool, St. Annes and Lytham Tramway Company Limited. Following the opening of new bus services in the 1960s, the Promenade route was the only commercial electric tramway left in the country. Today, Blackpool's tram system is rivalled only by Manchester's Metrolink and the Sheffield Super Trams.

Many of Blackpool's unique 'streamline' trams date from the 1930s or 50s, and the Tramway Company has a fleet of vintage cars used for special occasions, such as the autumn Illuminations. But there are also comfortable modern vehicles which make a trip out to Cleveleys or Fleetwood - a delightful experience. It's possible to combine a tram ride with a walk along the foreshore to enjoy surprisingly fine coastline views, with excellent birdlife including a variety of seabirds, waders, and at certain times of the year, wild duck and geese.

Further south along the coast lies **Lytham St. Annes**, a name synonymous with golf, for this peaceful resort boasts four magnificent championship courses attracting major tournaments each year.

What first strikes holiday-makers and visitors to Lytham St. Annes is the sensation of not knowing whether you are in one or two towns. There are in fact two towns here, Lytham and St. Annes-on-Sea, one is ancient and steeped in history while the other is relatively modern. It seems incredible that St. Annes, whose array of mixed architectural styles belies its true age, was a forerunner of Britain's garden cities created from a wilderness of sand dunes inhabited mainly by rabbits.

The sandy beaches here are a sunbather's paradise, as well as being ideal for a variety of sports, with sand yachting proving one of the most popular. However, Lytham is also renowned for its delightful parks, attractive gardens and beautiful floral displays. The atmosphere here is so relaxed that you can stroll unhurried, exploring the streets of the handsome town centre with its splendid shops, and pausing at one of the many quaint tearooms. You can even indulge in a little childhood reminiscence at the Toy and Teddy Bear Museum!

One place that is rapidly gaining a reputation for first class food and plenty of it, is **Rigby's Farmhouse Restaurant** in **Warton**, a hidden place well worth seeking out. Travelling out of Lytham along the A584, turn right into Church Road opposite the British Aerospace main gate and follow this road round a left hand bend into Carr Lane. Rigby's can be found on the right hand side. A working dairy farm run by the Rigby family, the 16th century farmhouse has been converted into a lovely restaurant, full of atmosphere and warmth, with beamed ceilings and open log fires in the lounge creating a cosy farmhouse feel. The food is simply wonderful - the best of English fare cooked to perfection, with interesting sauces adding an extra touch. The extensive menu includes such delights as Aberdeen Angus Steak and Roast Duckling Breast, but be warned, the Farmhouse Mixed Grill is a challenge for the heartiest appetite!

Rigby's Farmhouse Restaurant, Little Carrside Farm, Carr Lane, Warton Tel: 0772 632370

Not far from **Kirkham**, on the B5259, is the village of Wrea Green. A frequent winner of Lancashire's best kept village it is reminiscient of a by-gone age with its duck pond and cricket square.

The Grapes Hotel, Ribby Road, Wrea Green, near Kirkham Tel: 0772 682927

In a lovely setting, overlooking the village green, is **The Grapes Hotel**. This is a cosy pub and restaurant with a very friendly atmosphere. Part of the restaurant area is divided into quiet alcoves and the rest is open and conservatory style. The food is excellent and wide ranging, with children's menu and several vegetarian options. A particular novelty is Henry's Grillstone. The specially imported stones are heated to 300°C in the kitchen and then brought to your table for you to cook your meat yourself. Among the usual Boddington beers, there are also hand pulled and cask ales.

If you love fine food, you would be well advised to seek out **The Cromwellian Restaurant** which lies on the main street in the town of Kirkham, just a short walk from the market square. Built during the 17th century, it was originally a 3-storey town house, but today is a superb restaurant, acclaimed in various prestigious good food guides and with a comprehensive, award-winning wine list. Also a winner of the Restaurant of the Year award, it offers the discerning gastronome a tempting mix of both traditional and more unusual English fayre, with a three course menu offering five choices at each course, which changes monthly. Downstairs there are two small and cosy dining rooms with low beamed ceilings and traditional cottage style furnishings creating an intimate ambience in which to dine. After dinner you can retire to the comfortable coffee lounge upstairs for coffee and liqueurs.

The Cromwellian Restaurant, 16 Poulton Street, Kirkham
Tel: 0772 685680

Situated in the village of **Eaves**, on Eaves Lane is the the appropriately named **The Plough** at Eaves. Originally a 17th century coaching house, it is now home to a pub and restaurant run by Geoff Moss. The pub has a very cosy feel and the oldest room has very low ceilings with exposed beams and horse brasses. Old shotguns hang over the fireplace which houses real, open log fires in Winter. The restaurant and bar area are a more recent addition but still in keeping with the quaint country pub style. Excellent hand pulled beers are

112

available and there is a good menu, for the restaurant and the bar, with daily specials. There is also a separate pool room with traditional pub games. The restaurant is open lunchtimes and evenings and on Sundays, but closed on Mondays and Tuesdays. A unique tradition here, that goes back many years, is the roasting of chestnuts on the open fires, Saturday afternoons from October to December.

The Plough at Eaves, Eaves Lane, Eaves, Nr. Woodplumpton
Tel: 0772 690233

It is a relatively short distance from here to the Lancashire's administrative capital, **Preston** which makes a fine central point from which to explore the whole region. It is a town of ancient history, strategically situated on the highest navigable point of the River Ribble. It is still an active port, with cargo vessels and even an occasional special passenger boat, though most maritime activity nowadays comes from sailing and windsurfing in the Riversway Marina.

There is an impressive range of public buildings. The Parish Church occupies a site which has been in use for christian worship since the 7th century, and the present church has an elegant 205 foot high spire which soars above the town centre. **Preston Town Hall** was designed by Gilbert Scott in suitable Gothic style, whilst the fine **Harris Art Gallery, Museum and Library**, in equally impressive neo-classical style, provides a civic focal point close to the busy covered markets. The Harris Gallery has, incidentally, some of the most impressive collections of sculpture and paintings in the county.

In the centre of Preston, on the main shopping street is **Brucciani's**, a traditional café owned for many years by the Brucciani family but now part of the Café Inns chain. The Decor is reminiscent of an Italian Café in the 1920's and the staff even wear a black uniform with a white apron. The coffee and sandwiches are excellent, with a wide range of unusual fillings and bread rolls that literally melt in your mouth. This café bubbles with life at any time, but be warned, it gets very busy on Saturdays.

Brucciani's, Fishergate, Preston Tel: 0772 52406

Preston also has a number of covered shopping centres and pedestrianised areas, including the Guild Hall and Charter Theatre Complex which host a wide variety of events from straight theatre to classical and pop music and sporting events.

A famous event which takes place here is the **Preston Guild**, originally a celebration of restrictive practices which later became a fashionable bun-fight for the nobs and is now Britain's biggest carnival, celebrated every 20 years by an entire town. The Preston Guild merchant has an ancient and colourful tradition dating back more than 800 years. But what, you might ask, is its unusual event, from which derives the saying, "Once every Preston Guild", and what kind of appeal can span so many centuries?

The first Guilds were formed in Anglo-Saxon times as people grouped together for help and protection, but as trade and wealth increased, the "Guild Merchants" came into being. It is not known precisely when Preston's own Guild Merchant was established, but there is proof of a Preston Charter as early as 1179, and there may well have been a charter as early as 1100, 34 years after the Norman conquest.

Preston's merchants not only benefited from the exclusive trading rights they were granted and the freedom from tolls, but they also employed the Guild Merchant as a vehicle to ensure the quality control of Preston goods. Special Officers were appointed to see that cloth, for example, came up to a very exacting standard, that bread was baked to a specific size, and ale brewed to a given strength and sold at a prescribed price. Orders made under the Guild Merchant

114

powers ensured that the cottagers could buy in the market before the larger buyers came in, and all merchandise had to be sold in the open and within sight of the market cross - no doubt a reminder of people's Christian duty to one another.

With all this good fortune the merchants and people of Preston had plenty of reasons to celebrate and they set about creating the first Preston Guild ceremonies. However, you have a long wait until the next one, it isn't until 2012!

Worden Arts and Crafts Centre, Worden Park, Leyland, Lancashire
Tel: 0772 455908

It's only a short drive south of Preston to Worden Hall, **Leyland**. **The Worden Arts and Craft Centre** is surrounded by 157 acres of parkland and can be found just off the B5243. Opened in 1984, the Centre occupies the remaining buildings of Worden Hall, home of the Farrington family until 1947. The Centre houses a fully equipped theatre, craft workshops and a coffee shop. It is fascinating to watch crafts such as Pyrography, Woodturning, Knitting, Ceramics, Photography, Landscape Painting, Stained Glass and Blacksmithying in the process of being worked on.

Adjacent to the centre is the Lancashire branch of the Council for the Protection of Rural England, a registered charity which seeks to improve, protect and conserve the countryside. CPRE has a gift shop and an exhibition area, which features permanent displays of Worden Hall 'Then and Now'.

The main features of Worden Park include a 17th century ice house, a miniature railway, victorian maze, a garden for the blind, an arboretum, miniature golf, a children's play area, and several picnic areas. There is ample parking which is free in the main car park, and in the Centre car park. Coach parties are also welcome, but prior notice is requested. In the winter months visitors are advised to

Scarisbrick Hall, near Southport

telephone before visiting individual workshops.

Leyland is a small town, and it has seen a lot of changes in the last 20 years. In many ways, despite the demise of the commercial vehicle industry which previously dominated it, it has moved into a period of renewed prosperity and taken on a more leisurely and attractive character.

The town seems reluctant to give up its past, and has a **British Commercial Vehicle Museum** to attract today's visitors. The museum is housed in the former Leyland South Works on King Street, where commercial vehicles were produced for many years. The museum is devoted to the history of British Commercial Vehicles and efforts are made to ensure that exhibits include representations of all major manufacturers. The museum is the largest of its kind in Europe with exhibits ranging from the horse-drawn era through to steam wagons and early petrol vehicles up to the present day. The evolution of road vehicles can be traced as they developed to meet the vast growth in demand for passenger, goods and delivery vehicles.

This area south of the Ribble estuary has a strong agricultural and industrial heritage. Many villages also have fine churches. Visit St, Michael's in **Much Hoole**. This church was erected in 1628 and is regarded as the home of the beginning of English astronomy. St. Mary's in Penwortham has a lovely setting on Penwortham Hill overlooking the Ribble. The site dates back to Roman times, and the church has a 14th century chancel and tower which is 'perpendicular period'. In Leyland itself, look out for St. Andrew's. It is a 900 year old parish church and has beautiful stained glass windows.

From here, we cross the Irish Sea to the Isle of Man for the next chapter.

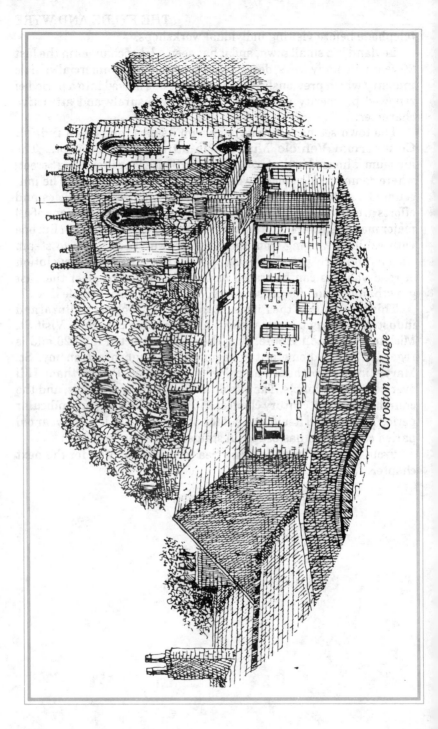

Croston Village

CHAPTER SIX

The Isle of Man

Cregneish Cottages

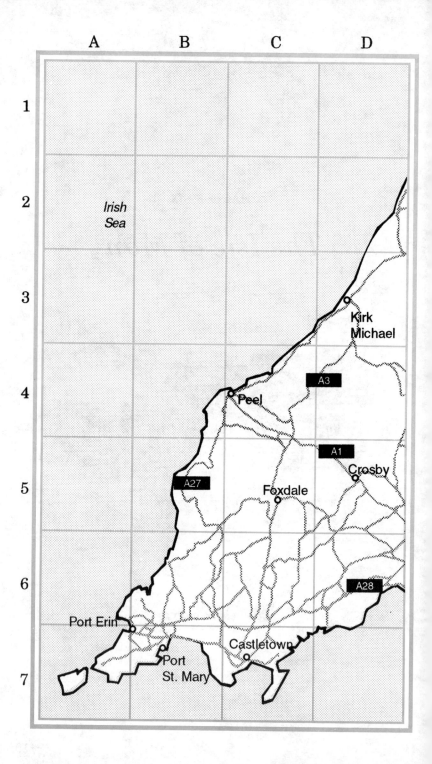

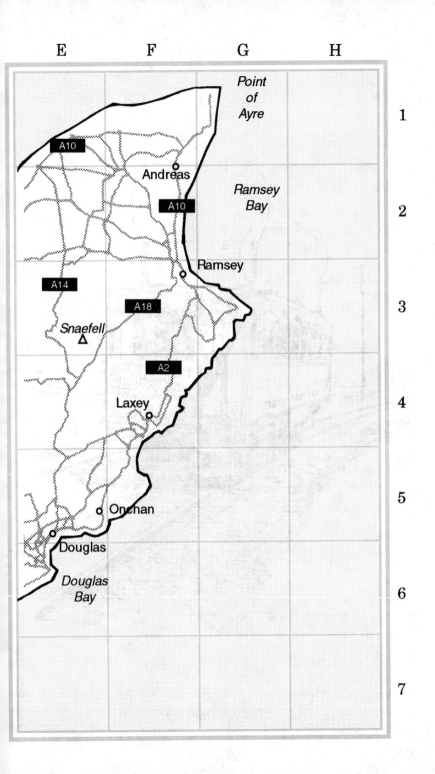

Snaefell Railway

CHAPTER SIX

The Isle of Man

The Isle of Man is perhaps best known for its annual T.T. motorcycle races, its tailless cat, Manx kippers and as a tax haven for the wealthy. However, there is much more to this beautiful island which, set in the heart of the Irish Sea, truly is a world apart. There are around 100 miles of coastline, encompassing eight major resorts, each one with its own individual character and appeal.

Getting here is much easier than you would expect. The island has its own airline, Manx Airlines, which operates a regular daily service from most UK airports and there are ferry services from Liverpool, Heysham and Fleetwood, as well as Belfast, Dublin and Stranraer.

This magical Isle became an island around 10,000 years ago when the meltwater of the Ice Age raised the sea level. Soon after this, the first people came, working and developing the island into the landscape we see today. The distinctive influences of the various different cultures who have lived here still remain, leaving a land with a unique and colourful heritage.

Among the first arrivals here were the Vikings. Evidence of this era, from the earliest chieftains to the last Norse King, abounds throughout the island. Against the skyline on the seaward side of the road between Ballaugh and Bride some early hilltop Viking burial mounds can be seen. At the ancient castle in Peel, an archaeological dig revealed many hidden Viking treasures which are now on display at the Manx Museum in the island's capital of Douglas, and at the Boathouse in Peel you can see a replica of the type of longship that brought the likes of Magnus Barefoot, Sigurd the Stout and Olaf the Dwarf.

Despite their reputation for plunder, rape and pillage, the Vikings also made some positive contributions to the island, not least of which was the establishment of the Manx governmental system, known as Tynwald. The Manx name of the Tynwald Hill is "Cronk Keeill Eoin", Hill of St. John's church. There is no record to confirm the story that it contains earth from all of the seventeen parish churches, but it is not unlikely that token portions of soil were added to the mound in accordance with an old Norse custom.

The Tynwald ceremony continues to this day with an annual

meeting of the Tynwald on Midsummer's Day at the ancient parliament field at St. Johns, where Manx citizens can petition parliament. Thus the Isle of Man is an independent country, with its own taxes, currency (British currency is also acceptable) and native language, although virtually everyone speaks English.

The famous three legged symbol seems to have been adopted in the 13th century as the amorial bearings of the native Kings of the Isle of Man, whose dominion also included the Hebrides. After 1266, when the native dynasty ended and control of the Island passed briefly to the Crown of Scotland and then permanently to the English Crown, the emblem was retained, and among the earliest survivng representations are those on the Manx Sword of State, thought to have been made in the year 1300 AD. The Three Legs also appeared on the Manx coinage of the seventeenth to nineteenth centuries, and are still seen in everyday use in the form of the official Manx flag.

Why the Three Legs were adopted as the Royal Arms of the Manx Kingdom is unknown. Many heraldic emblems had no meaning and were chosen merely because they were distinctive. This may have been the case with the Three Legs, though the emblem as such - like the cross and the swastika, to which it is related - has a long history reaching far back into pagan times. It was originally a symbol of the sun, the seat of Power and Life.

The motto incorporated with the Three Legs of Man on the official Coat of Arms is "Quocunque Jeceris Stabit", and means - "Whichever way you throw I shall stand".

Douglas, the island's capital is the obvious place to begin your tour and not surprisingly perhaps, is the liveliest of the resorts, its two-mile promenade being the focus of the island's nightlife. Live entertainment is provided at the Gaiety Theatre, Villa Marina and Summerland indoor leisure centre and there are numerous pubs, discos, cinemas, restaurants and amusement parks to choose from.

The 15 mile **Victorian Steam Railway** between Douglas and Port Erin provides a memorable journey along cliff tops, through bluebell woods and between steep-sided rocky cuttings, and serves as a reminder of a system that once served the whole island. The long steep climb out of Douglas produces loud puffing, smoke, soot and flying cinders, leaving little doubt that there is a steam engine at the front.

The **Manx Electric Railway** was one of the world's first when it opened in 1893. Today, the original electric tramcars still ply the 17 mile route between Douglas and Ramsey. The closed and open tramcars whistle and grind their way through leafy glens and hollows, before emerging on top of precipitous cliffs, offering spectacular view towards the Cumbrian coast.

Groudle Glen

125

From dawn to dusk you can enjoy a more leisurely ride along the magnificent sweep of Douglas Promenade aboard the **Douglas Bay Horse Tramway**, a remarkable and beautiful reminder of a bygone era. The history began when a civil engineer, Thomas Lightfoot, retired to the Isle of Man and, seeing the need for a public transport system along the promenade, designed the tramway. That the Douglas line has survived into the 1990s is remarkable. during the 1900s attempts were made to electrify the line and extend the Manx electric railway along the promenade - the plans were later dropped. A story often told about the horses that pull the trams, concerns a parrot that lived in a cage in a hotel close to a tram stop. The bird learnt to mimic the sound of the tram's starting bell and used to practise this skill constantly. The tram horses would stop when they heard the bell and immediately start again before passengers could alight. Result, chaos!

Scott's Bistro, 7 John Street, Douglas Tel: 0624 623764

Tucked up a little side street, close to the centre of Douglas you will discover an excellent place to eat called **Scott's Bistro**. This is the oldest house in Douglas and first received mention as far back as 1750. Its age and character are immediately apparent, with stoneflagged floors, oak beams and dark wooden furniture creating a cosy, olde worlde atmosphere. There is a ground floor and cellar restaurant and two further rooms upstairs which are available for private functions. In the summer months, the small courtyard provides a lovely outdoor setting in which to enjoy your meal. The Bistro has a well deserved reputation for the quality and variety of its food and owner Donald Slee has created an extensive menu which caters to every palate, ranging from light bites for visitors who just fancy a snack, to a choice of full meals all using the finest local produce and accompanied by a fine wine selection. This is definitely one of the Isle of Man's hidden gems.

126

When you're in the heart of Douglas, look out for the **Manx Cattery**. The Manx Cat, that has no tail, is probably the most famous export of the Isle of Man. One of the many delightful tales of how the cat lost its tail follows:

At the time that Noah built the Ark there were two Manx cats, both with tails. Noah sent for all the animals to come to the Ark two by two, but the Manx cats said "Oh, traa dy liooar" (which in Manx language means, time enough) and continued to play outside. Finally when they did decide to enter the Ark, Noah was just slamming the doors, and their tales were chopped off!

A variation on this story was that one cat reached the Ark safely but the other lost his tail when the door slammed shut. The tail-less one became the Manx cat, and the other became the infamous, grinning Cheshire Cat.

Not far from Douglas town centre, on Church Street, in one of the oldest parts of the town, you will find the **Rover's Return**. A particularly cosy establishment with a very traditional feel, perhaps due to the fact that it is the oldest pub in Douglas. Visitors should look out for the firemen's memorabilia including two brass and copper hose nozzles on the hand pumps. Real ales are served here with good food and a friendly welcome and the atmosphere is enhanced by the flagged floors and open fires. There is a courtyard beer garden to the rear. This pub, which incidentally is owned by Bushy's, the youngest brewery on the Isle of Man, is very popular with locals and visitors alike.

*Rover's Return, 11 Church Street, Douglas, Isle of Man Tel: 0624
676459*

One of the island's most famous landmarks is the Tower of Refuge

Eyreton Castle, Marown

which lies on the east coast of the island in Douglas Bay. Sir William Hilary, founder of the R.N.L.I., lived in a mansion overlooking the bay and, following a near-disaster on 20th November 1830 when the Royal Mail Steam Packet "St. George" was driven onto rocks in high seas, Hilary launched the Douglas lifeboat. Miraculously, all 22 crewmembers of the "St. George" and the lifeboat crew were saved, despite the treacherous conditions. It was after this incident that Hilary decided some sort of refuge was needed on Conister Rock for any shipwrecked mariners to shelter in. Thus the Tower of Refuge was built, with Hilary laying the foundation stone, appropriately enough on St. George's Day 1832. Since then, for more than 150 years, it has been used, though fortunately not often for its intended purpose.

Perched on a headland overlooking Douglas Bay is a **Camera Obscura**, known as the Great Union Camera. The camera was originally situated on the old iron pier, but when this was demolished in the 1870s the camera was re-sited on Douglas Head.

In a Camera Obscura natural daylight is focussed onto a white panel through a simple system of a lens and angled mirror, providing a living representation of the scene outside. At first apparently still, you soon become aware that the pictures are moving. The detail is remarkable, and it is often a wafting blade of grass or passing seagull which shows that this is no ordinary slideshow.

Manx National Heritage, British Isles Museum of the Year for 1992/3 has developed the "Story of Man". A dramatic and wide ranging portrayal of the unique history of the island. The journey of discovery begins at the Manx Museum in Douglas, and a visit here is a must during your stay.

At the "Island's Treasure House" in Douglas you can see the highly acclaimed Story of Man film, which introduces visitors to ten thousand years of turbulent history. The exciting gallery presentations which precede the film include the superb National Art Gallery, and describe the Story from the time of the 'Great Deer' to the present day, including the famous T.T. races and the Manx finance sector.

This showcase of Manx heritage is an invitation to begin a journey of discovery that will take you the length and breadth of the island. The Manx Museum is open Monday to Saturday. Admission is free and there is also a tea room, library and Heritage Shop.

Halfway between Douglas and Peel, on the main road at Greeba is a delightful place to eat in the form of **The Highlander** restaurant run by Stuart Deakin. We can vouch for both the food and service which are excellent and Stuart is an accomplished host. There is a cosy little lounge where you can have a drink while perusing the menu which is nicely balanced to give the more adventurous a new experience while retaining some 'classic' tastes. A good wine list complements the food. The restaurant is both intimate and welcoming with silver cutlery and linen tablecloths adding to the candelit atmosphere. This is an ideal place for a special occasion where you can relax and enjoy your evening without being rushed. Recommended.

Highlander Restaurant, Main Road, Greeba Tel: 0624 852870

If you are looking for a relaxing and comfortable holiday base from which to explore the delights of the Isle of Man, you would be well advised to seek out **Hillberry Manor**, a lovely Victorian gentleman's residence owned by Richard and Penny Leventhorpe who take great pleasure in inviting guests to their home. Richard is a direct descendant of the last independent Lord of Man and is a former representative of the House of Keys. Hillberry Manor can be found down a narrow lane through Hillberry, just above Onchan and stands in spacious grounds, surrounded by lovely countryside. In keeping with the age and character of the house, beautiful antiques and attractive furnishings lend an air of gracious country living. Very comfortable accommodation is provided in three well appointed guest rooms, two en-suite and one with private bathroom and each equipped with a useful information pack to help you make the most of your stay. Evening meals are provided by prior arrangement offering guests traditional English food cooked to gourmet standards and incorporating the best of Manx produce wherever possible.

Hillberry Manor, Little Mill, Onchan Tel: 0624 661660

Only two and a half miles north of Douglas is **Groudle Glen**. It is of a deep, and in places, rocky nature, with lively bubbling stream running through its length. Excellent specimens of beech grow in the upper section while lower done pines and larch are more abundant. A small water wheel is situated in the lower glen. An attraction in the Glen is the miniature railway run by enthusiasts, operating certain days only.

Despite its relatively small size, the Isle of Man really is the ideal holiday island, with a range of superb amenities, activities and events to suit every age group and pocket. There are various events throughout the year, ranging from Viking long boat races and vintage transport weekends, to the world renowned TT Motor Cycle Races and less well known and very wet World Tin Bath Championship!

Sporting facilities here are excellent, with clear seas and indoor pools for swimming, gentle pony trekking rides, and for the golfing enthusiast several championship courses, with some clubs offering special competitions to visitors.

Seven miles up the east coast from Douglas is the village of **Laxey**, set in a deep wooded glen. This is a village of interesting contrast. Tracing the river up from its mouth in a small tidal harbour and adjacent partially stoney beach, the route takes you past the woollen mill, tram terminus and on up to the Great Laxey Wheel marking the once thriving minig centre.

Laxey Glen is one of the Island's seventeen National Glens, maintained and preserved by the Forestry department of the Manx Government. There is no admission charge to any of the Glens, so be sure visit them, and enjoy the scenic beauty of the Manx countryside.

On the eastern coast of the island, set within the Agneash Valley between Douglas and Ramsey lies the village of Laxey. Here, standing proudly at the head of the Laxey Mines you will discover the famous Lady Isabella Wheel, the largest water wheel of its kind in the world. The circumference is a staggering 228 feet, the diameter 72 feet and the top platform stands some 72 feet above the ground.

It was Robert Casement, engineer to the mines, who constructed this mechanical wonder, designed to pump 250 gallons of water per minute from a depth of 200 fathoms. It was officially opened on 27th September 1854 and named Lady Isabella after the wife of the then Lieutenant Governor of the island.

Today, after considerable repairs and major reconstruction work, the Wheel functions exactly as it did over 100 years ago, creating a unique Victorian engineering feature and making this a centre for industrial archaeology. The viewing platform over the wheel is very popular with the more daring visitors, while others may enjoy the tranquility of the glen where the remains of one of the greatest lead mines can be seen. The wheel is open daily from Easter to the end of September and there is an admission charge.

The Laxey Wheel, Laxey, Isle of Man Tel: 0624 675522

Situated in a beautiful natural glen in the Manx hills, not far from Laxey, the **Ballalheannagh gardens** are given a star in the Best Gardens of Great Britain, which puts them among the top in the country . Any visitor who is interested in gardening or just in the beauty of nature will find these gardens a delight. Steep winding paths cling to the valley sides and crystal water cascades below carry the bells of pieris to the Irish Sea. The valley is packed with rhododendrons, shrubs, bulbs and ferns as well as much more unusual species. The Ballalheannagh Gardens, created by the owners Clif and Maureen Dadd, are in effect gardens to visit with a nursery from which you can also buy. The Dadds maintain an extensive catalogue of unusual plants which can be seen growing in their natural habitat. The Gardens are in a very well hidden spot, but one which is worth seeking out.

Ballalheannagh Gardens, Glen Roy, Lonan Tel: 0624 781875

The island has a surprisingly varied and unspoilt landscape. From the northern lowlands with their seemingly endless sandy beaches to the delicate flora of the central moorlands, from mountainous and rugged fell country which rewards the stalwart walker with spectacular views, to the dramatic cliffs and coves of the southern seascape - a haven for a myriad of sea birds who make their nests here - the Isle of Man is a walker's paradise.

The northernmost resort of the Isle of Man is **Ramsey**, an attractive coastal town with a snug harbour which is highly regarded by visiting yachtsmen. Once ashore you will find a rich variety of bars, restaurants and fine shops in which to browse at your leisure. A short walk out of town will take you to the Mooragh Park and the Rural Life Museum, both of which are well worth a visit.

Just 1 mile north of Ramsey is the **Grove Rural Life Museum**. A pleasantly proportioned, time capsule Victorian house, the Grove Museum was developed as a summer retreat for Duncan Gibb, a Victorian shipping merchant from Liverpool and his family. The rooms, from drawing room to scullery, retain their period furnishings, augmented with displays of toys and costumes. The outbuildings house an interesting collection of vehicles and agricultural instruments appropriate to the larger Manx farms of the 19th century.

Take time to stroll through the beautifully maintained gardens, complete with ducks and Manx cats! The museum is open from Easter to the end of September and there is an admission charge.

One of only three Deluxe graded bed and breakfast establishments on the island, **Poyll Dooey House** is probably the most hidden of the three, yet lies only a few minutes walk from Ramsey. To get here, turn

Laxey Wheel

off Lezayre Road (the A3 to Peel) onto Gardeners Lane and continue as far as the ford where you turn right into Poyll Dooey and the house lies about 100 yards further up on the right.

Poyll Dooey House, Gardeners Lane, Ramsey Tel: 0624 814684

Dating back to the 17th century, Poyll Dooey House has previously been a gentleman's residence and a private school for girls. It was once owned by a relative of Fletcher Christian, who gained renown for instigating the mutiny on the Bounty. Today it is the charming home of David and Anne Greenwood, who enjoy sharing it with their many guests. The house stands in an acre and a half of lovely grounds, adjacent to a 40 acre nature reserve. Very comfortable accommodation is provided in three luxuriously appointed bedrooms, one of which boasts a four poster bed. Two are ensuite and one has a private bathroom. The Greenwoods also provide 5 keys deluxe self-catering accommodation in a splendid 15th century converted corn mill which enjoys a clifftop location on the beautiful west coast.

Just three miles from Ramsey, in the north of the Isle of Man, lies **Kerrowmoar House**, a magnificent Georgian property, completely hidden from a busy road accessible only by a meandering drive flanked with flowering trees and paddocks. This secluded gem, with its own indoor, heated swimming pool, and all-weather tennis court is also the comfortable family home of Diana and Fred Parkes offering two star deluxe Bed and Breakfast accommodation to those lucky enough to stumble across it.

There are three comfortable double rooms, each with television, telephone and tea-making facilities, and two guest bathrooms and a shower room. Kerrowmoar House is ideally situated for exploring the beautiful Manx countryside and picnics can be provided.

Kerrowmoar House, Sulby, Lezayre, Ramsey, Isle of Man
Tel: 0624 897543 Fax: 0624 897927

Diana and Fred also have two self-catering cottages and an apartment at **Thie Hene** in **Ballaugh** and **Park View** in **Kirk Michael**. Both are well equipped and have a pay phone, garden with barbeque and ample car parking. A nice touch is that the Parkes leave milk, bread, butter and eggs to welcome guests on arrival.

Thie Hene, Main Street, Ballaugh, Isle of Man

Travelling inland from Ramsey, family members of all ages will enjoy a trip to **Curragh's Wildlife Park** which lies between Sulby and Ballaugh. Officially opened in 1965, this magnificent park aims to educate, stimulate and entertain the thousands of visitors who come here each year. It also plays a crucial role in animal welfare and the conservation of endangered species.

135

Since it opened, the Park has succeeded in achieving its ultimate aim, that is, that all the animals are breeding. This is true of all species of mammals and most species of bird currently at the Park, including the only breeding colony of Scarlet Ibis in the British Isles. One of the major attractions has to be the magnificent walk through the aviary with birds of every colour and description. From the café you can enjoy the beautiful sight of the flamingo beach and main lake, where these beautiful pink birds offset perfectly the backdrop of the blue lake and green hills.

Another popular attraction is the 'Tantalising Ten', a group of ten Canadian and Small Clawed otters whose antics in their own private 'swimming pools' provide hours of amusement for visitors of all ages. Of course no visit here would be complete without witnessing feeding time, with penguins and pelicans being fed at 11.00am and 3.00pm and the sea-lions who put on quite an act for their audience, being fed at 11.30pm and 3.30pm.

On the western side of the island lies **Peel**. It is generally felt that Peel, renowned for its sometimes spectacular sunsets, typifies tthe unique character and atmosphere of the Isle of Man. Traditionally the centre of the Manx fishing industry, including the delicious oak smoked kippers and fresh shellfish, Peel has managed to avoid any large scale developments. Its narrow winding streets exude history and draw the visitor unfailingly down to the harbour, sandy beach and magnificent castle in local red sandstone.

Peel Castle, one of the Isle of Man's principal historic monuments, occupies the important site of St. Patrick's Isle at Peel. The Castle's imposing Curtain Wall encircles the ruins of the many buildings, including St. Patrick's Church and the Round Tower from the 11th century, the 13th century Cathedral of St. German, and the later apartments of the Lords of Man.

In the 11th century the Castle became the ruling seat of the Norse Kingdom of Man and the Isles, first united by Godfred Crovan - the King Orry of Manx folklore.

Recent archaeological excavation has discovered exciting new evidence relating to the long history of the site. One of the most dramatic finds was the Norse period grave of a lady of high social status buried in pagan splendour. The jewellery and effects buried with her can be seen on display with other excavation finds at the Manx Museum in Douglas, while a walk beneath the Castle's brooding walls will instil something of the strength and history of this great natural fortress.

The museum is open daily from Easter to the end of September and there is an admission charge.

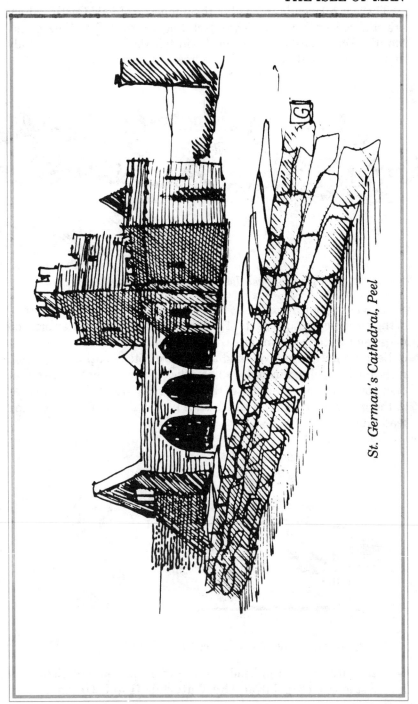

St. German's Cathedral, Peel

There is a legend attached to the dungeons of Peel Castle, which are said to be haunted by The Black Dog, or to use its Manx name, Mauthe Dhoo. The people of Peel will tell you that on dark windy nights you can still hear howling across the harbour.

Peel Castle, Peel, Isle of Man Tel: 0624 675522

Travelling south from Peel, the village of **Glen Maye** has to be one of the most picturesque parts of the Isle of Man. A spectacular bridged gorge and waterfall dominate this glen, which is some 3 miles south of Peel. Comprising eleven and a half acres, its beautiful sheltered, fern-filled woodland includes some relics of the ancient forests that once covered Man. A feature of this glen is the "Mona Erin", another of the many water wheels which once provided power for the Manx lead mines. ·

The Waterfall Hotel, Glen Maye, Isle of Man Tel: 0624 842238

Here, situated at the head of the Glen itself you will discover a lovely stopping-off point at **The Waterfall Hotel**. Originally two cottages, one of which was reputedly a smuggler's cottage, this delightful pub lies only five minutes walk from the waterfall after which it was named and sitting outside in the summer you can enjoy magnificent views to a backdrop of rushing water. Winner of the Isle of Man pub section of Britain in Bloom 1993, The Waterfall's attractive exterior is matched by an interior where oak beams, dried flowers and open fires enhance a cosy, relaxed atmosphere. The pub has an excellent reputation for food with a varied menu of tasty bistro style meals to appeal to every palate, which makes it a popular venue with locals and visitors alike.

Of course there is no better way to work off your lunchtime excesses than by striding out along the footpaths to the waterfall itself, and absorbing the breathtaking scenery of this beautiful leafy glen and cascading mountain streams.

Ballacallin Hotel, Dalby, Patrick, Isle of Man Tel: 0624 842030

If you are looking for a place to stay, then continuing south along the A27, just beyond the village of **Dalby** the **Ballacallin Hotel** makes a super touring base and despite its name is very much a country inn with rooms. Voted one of CAMRA's top pubs on the island, the Ballacallin was originally an 18th century farmhouse which has been extended over the years. Its super hillside location looking out to the sea affords guests the most spectacular views. Recently refurbished, the hotel is attractively furnished in traditional farmhouse style and provides very comfortable accommodation in eight en-suite guest rooms. You can relax in the lounge bar where a coal burning stove enhances a cosy atmosphere and on fine days you can enjoy a drink out on the sun terrace with its amazing seascape views. The food here is excellent, all homecooked and mostly using local produce - the traditional fish and chips served here are reputedly the best on the island!

If ever the words 'safe haven' applied they must surely belong to

Port Erin's beach. Situated between magnificent headlands. The sand is soft and cleaned daily, there are rock pools to one side and a quay to the other. Sitting on the beach can be a day dreamers paradise, watching the world go by - maybe the RNLI lifeboat will indulge you in a practise launch whilst you are there. When the guilt born of inactivity overcomes you, a walk up to Bradda Glen and its licensed café bar with garden tables is recommended.

The **Falcon's Nest Hotel** can be found on the promenade at **Port Erin**. Owned by Bob and Loretto Potts, this imposing, ornate building, formerly home to the Trustrum family, has been converted into a wonderful hotel. The Potts' work is ongoing in an attempt to return the whole building to its original condition.

Falcon's Nest Hotel, The Promenade, Station Road, Port Erin,
Isle of Man Tel: 0624 834077

The bedrooms are being restored and furnished with traditional items. The original ballroom with a beautifully ornate ceiling, is used as a function room and second restaurant and features a Carvery every Saturday night. The bar is wood panelled, has a cosy atmosphere and is known to the locals as Porky's Bar - after the portly barman who runs it. The main restaurant is large and airy and offers expansive sea views and with the bars is open to non-residents. There is also a coffee shop which is open all day to non-residents and offers light snacks. The hotel has a fantastic location on the cliff-top and has commanding views over the sea. Particular care has been taken to preserve the exterior appearance, even down to the specially commissioned wrought iron balustrades and lamps.

The south of the island has a lot to offer the keen explorer. Perched right on the south western tip, **Cregneash Village Folk Museum** offers a unique experience of Manx traditional life within a 19th century crofting village. Overlooking the small island and bird

140

sanctuary known as the Calf of Man, **Cregneash** is isolated from the rest of the island and was one of the last strongholds of the traditional skills and customs which characterised the crofters' way of life.

Cregneash Village Folk Museum, Cregneash, Isle of Man
Tel: 0624 675522

By combining small scale farming with other occupations, a small community of Manx men and women have successfully prospered here since the middle of the 17th century and in the carefully preserved buildings at the southern end of the village you can see the conditions in which they lived and marvel at the tenacity of spirit which must have sustained them in their rugged lifestyle.

The centre-piece of the village is without doubt **Harry Kelly's Cottage**. Kelly was a renowned Cregneash crofter and fluent speaker who died in 1934. The cottage provided the starting point of the Museum when it opened to the public in 1938 and much of Harry's own furniture and other equipment is on display here.

There are various other buildings of interest, such as the Turner's Shed, The Smithy and The Karran Farm, all inviting exploration. Cregneash is also one place on the island where you will see the unusual Manx Loaghtan four-horned sheep, a breed which, thanks to the development of two healthy flocks by Manx National Heritage, has been preserved for the foreseeable future.

The museum is open daily from Easter to the end of September and there is an admission charge.

If you like boats then don't miss **Port St. Mary** with its inner and outer harbour, two piers and with good anchorage for visiting yachts, it is very much a small working port. The beach here, just along the scenic walkway from the harbour, is no more than two miles from Port Erin beach and yet faces in almost the opposite direction, so finding a sheltered bay in this part of the Island is easy.

For lovers of cliff walks and coastal scenery, one of the finest walks in the Isle of Man is the route from Port St. Mary to Port Erin along the Raad ny Foillan (the road of the gull) - a long distance footpath around the perimeter of the island. The first part of the walk takes you to the Chasms - gigantic vertical rifts of varying width, descending in some places the whole height of the 400 feet high cliffs. Down below the Chasms is the Sugar-loaf rock, a huge detached sea stack of horizontal slate. Sugar-loaf rock is teaming with bird life, so keen photographers should take a telephoto lens to get good pictures.

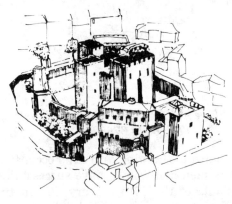

Castle Rushen, Castletown, Isle of Man Tel: 0624 675522

To the east, **Castletown** is the original capital of the island, its harbour lying beneath the imposing battlements of the finely pre-served **Castle Rushen**. Like Peel Castle, this too is said to be haunted, by a ghost known as The White Lady. Believed to be the ghost of Lady Jane Gray who travelled to the island from Scotland with her family over 100 years ago, she has been seen walking the battlements at night and occasionally walking through the closed Main Gate of the castle during the day.

The castle itself dates back to around 1153 when Norsemen began its construction. A series of fascinating displays bring the history and atmosphere of this great fortress vividly to life, presenting in authen-tic detail the sights, sounds and smells of a bygone era. Among its various points of interest is a unique one-fingered clock, which was presented by Queen Elizabeth I in 1597 and still keeps perfect time. Operated by a series of ropes and pulleys, it has to be wound daily, a task quite often undertaken by one of the castle's many visitors.

Another place worth visiting in Castletown is the **Nautical Mu-seum** where a display centres on the late 18th century armed yacht 'Peggy' in her contemporary boathouse. Part of the original building is constructed as a cabin room of the Nelson period and the museum has various other displays of a nautical theme.

While you are driving around this corner of the Island, look out for the **Fairy Bridge**. For centuries, poeple in the Isle of Man have taken no chances when it comes to the little people. Tales of the 'Bugganes' and the 'Mauthe Dhoo' live on in the minds of the Manx people, and the 'cross cern' fashioned from the branch of a Rowan tree still guards against eveil spirits over each and every doorway. But few pagan customs seem to have such a hold as that of bidding Good Morning to the fairies that live under Ballalona Bridge, it is thought to bring you luck!

Bushy's Brewery and The Hop Garden, Mount Murray, Braddan,
I.O.M. Tel: 0624 661244

Situated on **Mount Murray**, on the A5 Douglas to Castletown road, is **Bushy's Brewery** the newest brewery on the Isle of Man and a fascinating place to visit, for here visitors can observe the complete brewing process. The brewery even has its own hop garden so you really can see the initial raw fruit being made into beer. There is even provision for visitors to sample the finished product! Next door to the brewery is a pub, called appropriately enough, The Hop Garden (opens May 1994). It is a traditional style of pub where visitors can enjoy good food with a good pint from Bushy's. There is a patio and beer garden offering splendid views of the island and makes a perfect place to while away a few hours.

The island's pace of life is so easy that you can't help but relax. For a short break or a longer stay, the Isle of Man is a unique and fascinating holiday destination.

CHAPTER SEVEN

West Lancashire and Merseyside

Speke Hall

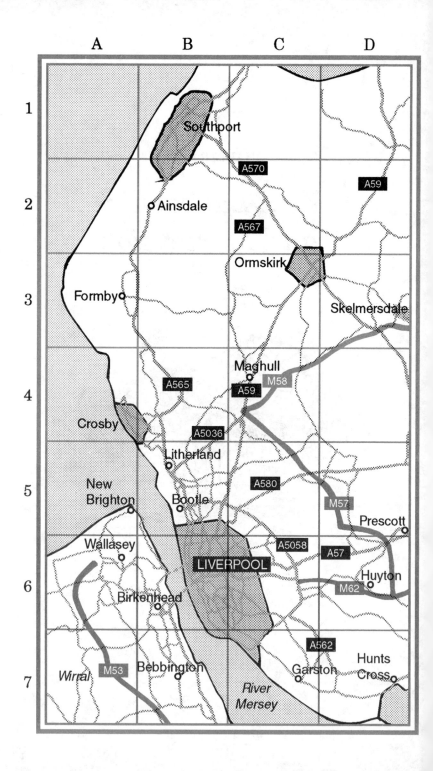

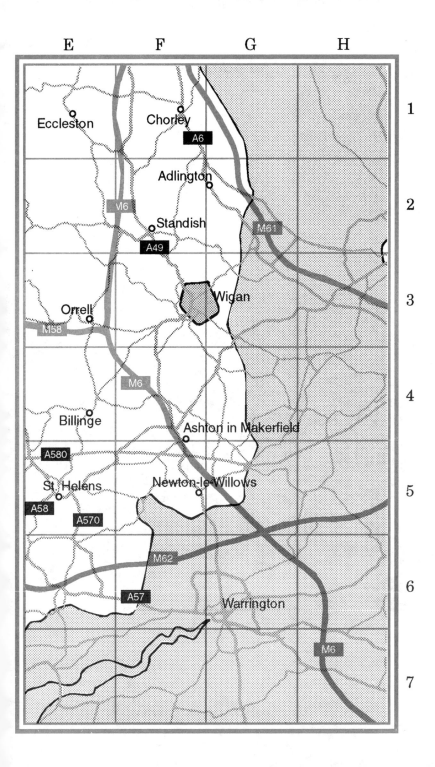

Blue Coat Chambers, Liverpool

West Lancashire and Merseyside

A bustling, friendly place, the Lancashire town of **Chorley** has always retained the friendly atmosphere of a market town, with its market dating back to 1498. Today there are two markets - the covered market and the open, 'Flat Iron' market. History breathes through thus intriguing name, which is derived from the ancient practice of trading by displaying goods on the ground without the use of stalls.

Momentous events in history have brushed Chorley; the Civil War brought fighting close by with the Battle of Preston Moor and retreating Royalist troops were twice engaged in battle by Cromwell's soldiers. The outcome was not happy one for the Royalist army, but it guaranteed Chorley a place in the history books.

Tangible evidence of Chorley's exciting and evocative past can be found in the wealth of architectural riches scattered throughout the borough. Look for the Parish Church of St. Laurence for example. It dates back to 1360 and the remains of St. Laurence are reputedly enshrined there. Miles Standish, the courageous Captain of the New England Puritans who sailed to America on the Mayflower, is remarkable for a modern-day puzzle. His personal records in this church now seem to have been deleted, shedding doubt on his supposed connection with the Standishes of Duxbury, prominent local gentry.

Chorley also has strong associations with sugar, being the birthplace of Henry Tate in 1819. He was the founder of the world famous Tate & Lyle sugar refiners and benefactor of the art galleries across England that now bear his name, The Tate Galleries.

The jewel of Chorley is without doubt **Astley Hall**. Built around 1580 and set within beautiful parkland, it is regarded as a fine Elizabethan mansion. Extended in 1666, and later in 1825, it is truly a house with a history. The rooms reflect the passage of centuries, containing fine furniture from 1600 to the Edwardian period. The Hall was given to Borough in 1922 by Reginald Tatton, and it was he who insisted that it should incorporate a memorial to those who died in World War I. So, there is a small room in Astley Hall which displays the names and the photographs and the Books of Remembrance and

149

relatives still come to find the record and to remember.

The truly remarkable ceilings in the Great Hall and the drawing room, thought to be the best examples of their kind in England, display the skills of those who created masterpieces in plaster. Then, of course, there is the Cromwell mystery - and his boots. Did he stay here or not? The case can be argued both ways. Intriguing questions abound about Astley Hall. But one thing is certain. Many of those who visit often fall in love with its atmosphere.

So it comes across as a home, not as a static collection of things from the past. And that is exactly the effect the staff strive to achieve. Astley Hall, alive with bustle and people in 1580, lives on today and waits to welcome you.

Astley Hall, Astley Park, Chorley Tel: 0257 262166

Just outside Chorley, on the other side of Junction 8 on the M61 are the villages of **Upper** and **Lower Wheelton**. Divided into two parts, this pleasantly laid out village is situated on the main Chorley-Blackburn road. Its tiny streets climb in slopes, giving an accurate impression of the surrounding hilly countryside. The locks on the Leeds Liverpool Canal are a fascinating reminder of the canal link that was once so vital.

A little further towards Blackburn off the A674 is Withnell Fold Village. It was built to house the workforce of the nearby paper mill, by the Parke family. This idyllic little village of terraced cottages and tiny houses, stone-built mills and impressive village square is almost certainly one of the most attractive in the country. Withnell Fold was, in latterday times, a famous exporter of banknote paper to the world.

Lying on the western edge of the West Pennine Moors, south of Chorley and on the eastern side of the M61, is **Lever Park**. Situated on the lower slopes of Rivington Moor was made over as a gift to the general public in 1902, by William Hesketh Lever, later Lord Leverhulme and eventually Viscount Leverhulme. Lever Park comprises a awe-inspiring pot-pourri of ornamental, landscaped gardens, tree lined avenues, cruck framed barns, a Georgian Hall and a treasure trove of natural history exhibits extending to over 2,000 acres. Lever Park's moorland setting, elevated position and adoining reservoirs provide scenery on a grand scale which leaves a lasting impression.

The nearby village of **Rivington** is charming and is surrounded by moorland of outstanding natural beauty and interest. Rivington Pike is 1,191 feet above sea level and was originally the site of a signal beacon. Before returning to Chorley, the Lead Mines Clough on Anglezarke Moor shouldn't be missed.

To the west of Chorley by the little River Yarrow, you will find the delightful, award-winning village of **Croston** - now a conservation area - which has some 17th century almshouses and a lovely 15th century church. Strong links with agriculture and farming are still apparent in this area and the open farmlands actually extend right into the centre of the village.

For self-catering enthusiasts, **Cockfight Barn** in Croston is a rare gem. This 250 year old brick built barn has been recently converted to provide excellent self-catering accommodation, but still retains its original character and charm. Most of the accommodation is on the first floor and boasts outstanding countryside views. Every modern amenity has been provided for maximum comfort during your holiday, including a washing machine, tumble dryer, fridge/freezer, dishwasher and microwave. Cockfight Barn is managed by Red Rose Cottages - telephone 0200 27310 for a brochure.

Cockfight Barn, Manor House Farm, Croston, Near Preston
Tel: 0200 27310

To the south, and just off the A59 lies **Rufford**, an attractive village of white walled houses notable for its church and its old and new halls. The church was built in 1869 and is a splendid example of the Gothic revival period with its modern coloured glass and tall spire that dominates the skyline. The new village hall provides the venue for a host of community activities. There is also an annual May Fair held on the Village Green which celebrates a charter granted by Elizabeth I in 1573 and retains a charming medieval atmosphere.

Situated at the north end of the village, Rufford Old Hall is without doubt one of the finest examples of 15th century architecture in Lancashire. Particularly noted for its magnificent Great Hall, this impressive black and white timbered building invites exploration. From the superb, intricately carved movable wooden screen to the solid oak chests and long refectory table, the atmosphere here is definitely one of wealth and position. Within outbuildings, you will find the Philip Ashcroft Museum of Rural Life, a National Trust property which houses a unique collection of items which illustrate fully village life in pre-industrial Lancashire. There is also a popular restaurant and a shop where you will find the perfect memento of your visit.

Rufford Old Hall, Rufford, Near Ormskirk Tel: 0704 821254

The nearby village of Mawdesley is well worth a quick visit as it is a past winner of the 'Best Kept Village in Lancashire'. Again, this is a village devoted mainly to agricultural pursuits, but it was once associated with a thriving basket making industry, founded 150 years ago. Mawdesley Hall, thought to have been erected by William Mawdesley in 1625 is worthy of some architectural note, as is the school.

If you are a keen birdwatcher and nature lover, then your next port of call should definitely be **Martin Mere Wildfowl and Wetlands Centre** which lies north of **Burscough**. Set within 363 acres of marshland, this excellent nature reserve plays a vital role in the conservation of 120 different species of geese, ducks and swans, some of which are very rare and unusual, but tame enough to be fed from the hand. The excavation of a large lake and development of several ponds has created the ideal habitat for the 1600 resident birds. From the unique Norwegian log Visitor Centre with its turfed roof which blends in so well with the landscape, you can look out on the Swan Lake and Flamingo Pool from the viewing concourse or take time to browse through the Exhibition Hall and picture gallery. Outside, the acres of fine landscaped gardens are a joy to stroll around and a peaceful nature trail also links nine birdwatching hides, where you can see wild flower and plants, woodland birds, butterflies and other insects.

Rufford Old Hall

Billinge Church, Southport

Added to all this is a café, shop and ample free parking and almost all of the Centre is accessible to wheelchairs and buggies, which makes Martin Mere an ideal place to spend a day out.

Travelling south along the A59 you will come to Burscough, a semi-urban area located between Ormskirk and Rufford. The village adorns the Leeds to Liverpool canal which passes through the parish. Burscough Parish Church was one of the Million, or Waterloo Churches, built as a thanks offering after the final defeat of Napolean in 1815. A later addition to the church was a memorial window to those who gave their lives in the First World War.

The crumbling ruins of **Burscough Priory** lie strewn along Abbey Lane, adjacent to the A59. Although scheduled as an ancient monument, only very small parts of some walls remain. It was founded for the Black Canons in the early 12th century and subsequently received such lavish endowments that it became one of the most important religious houses in Lancashire.

A little further south, along the A59, is the pleasant market town of **Ormskirk** which has some interesting 18th century and Victorian buildings - shops, inns and public buildings, as well as some attractive terraced houses of the same period. There is an excellent shopping centre here, much of which is pedestrianised and on Thursdays and Saturdays is converted into an open air market. Dating back some 700 years, the market continues a tradition which owes its existence to the Burscough Priory Monks. It was during the reign of King Edward I (1272-1307) that a Charter was granted to the Monks to hold a weekly market which to this day is a browser's delight, with a wide range of stalls selling everything from fish, meat, and vegetables to clothing, china and bric-a-brac.

Keep an eye out for two houses on Greetby Hill, Balaclava Villa and Inkerman Lodge in rememberance of the Crimean War. Their gate-posts are topped with real cannon balls!

Ormskirk Parish Church is an architectural gem and is almost unique among Parish Churches by having both a spire and a separate tower. Originally dating back to the 12th century there is evidence of Saxon, Celtic and Norman work. The building was used by the local nobility including the Stanleys, the Scarisbricks, the Earl of Derby and his step-son King Henry VII. All have left their mark on the chapel.

For some gentle relaxation in a peaceful setting, why not visit **Beacon Country Park**, just outside Ormskirk. The Park boasts a superb Golf Course and driving range, walking trails, a pizzeria where you can indulge in the finest Sicilian pizzas, and a relaxing bar - all of which adds up to 360 acres of pure enjoyment.

Between Ormskirk and Maghull, the village of **Aughton** is considered one of the most attractive residential districts in the area, its tree-lined roads and fine village hall enhancing its carefully preserved natural beauty. There are two churches, Christ Church and St. Michaels, both of which are of particular architectural interest.

To the west, if you travel to Southport along the A570, you will pass through **Scarisbrick**. The town is made up of restaurants, shops and houses, all straddled along the main road. There are also some fine farm buildings dating back to the last century. Horse riding is a popular sport here, and the canal provides ample opportunity for fishing, boating and walking.

Scarisbrick Hall is situated on the site of the ancestral home of the Scarisbrick family, which itself dated back to the time of King Stephen. The present building was completed in 1867 and is reputed to be the finest example of Gothic Revival Architecture in England. The turrets, gables and pinnacles are dwarfed by the slender, 100 foot tower, which bears a great resemblance to the clock tower of the Houses of Parliament. The last member of the family to live here was Sir Everard Scarisbrick who disposed of the Hall in 1945. It is now a boarding school.

To the west, the Lancashire coast rewards exploration handsomely, with its attractive seaside towns, lovely beaches and wealth of wildlife. **Southport** is, and remains one of Lancashire's most popular resorts. If it doesn't have quite the bravura of Blackpool, it does have style, with **Lord Street** and its arcades still being one of the region's most elegant shopping streets. Even though it is a seaside resort, you sometimes have to travel some distance across broad expanses of sand to reach the sea, and the pier is so long that a railway takes you out to the pier end, where at low tide the sea and the Mersey estuary can still be some way off. There is all that you would expect to find at a seaside resort: lots of sand (especially dunes), refreshments, funfairs, rides, walks, boating pools, toy trains and fine gardens, including superb herbaceous borders and dahlia beds in late summer. It is also worth travelling out from here to Hesketh Park or to the delightful **Botanic Gardens** at Meols Hall.

Situated on Lord Street in Southport, is the delightful **Atkinson Art Gallery** with superb collections of British Art, English glass and Chinese porcelain. Admission is free. On Derby Road you will find the Southport Railway Centre which has a large display of steam and diesel locomotives, housed in the old engine shed. Before leaving the area, the Botanic Gardens and Museum in Churchtown are well worth a visit. The gardens are a delight at any time of year and contain an aviary, fernery, bowling greens and children's playground. The

St. Luke's Church, Liverpool

Metropolitain Cathedral of Christ the King, Liverpool

museum houses an interesting display of Victoriana. Admission is free.

Further south along the coast, **Formby** is of national importance for its nature conservation interest - past **Birkdale**, also famous for its golf course, Ainsdale and into the Formby Hills, where pine woods flourish on the dunes. Lying between the Mersey and Ribble estuaries, Formby Point is an area of constant change where Man battles with the elements in an effort to prevent the merciless erosion of the coastline. The dunes protect the hinterland from flooding like a natural sea wall, but they also bring their own problems. Sand blown by storms has in the past threatened inland villages with engulfment and since around 1700, leaseholders in the area were required by law to plant marram grass to help stabilise the dunes. The woods were first planted at the beginning of this century for the same reason, and the intention was that an esplanade would be constructed along the coast if the sand could be held at bay.

The fact that Nature refuses to be so easily tamed has proved to be of great benefit to nature lovers who visit the area, as much of it is now a **National Nature Reserve**. Almost 500 acres of Formby's dunes and woodlands were bought by the National Trust in 1967, and it now provides a natural habitat for a wide range of animals and plants. Two animals in particular make Formby Point well known. The red squirrel colony descends from the variety introduced here from the Continent many years ago, and owes its success largely to being so well fed by visitors. The fact that so few trees grow on Formby's hinterland means that the colony is also well protected from its enemy, the grey squirrel, which is prevented access. The other animal which is eagerly looked for, but far more difficult to spot than the red squirrel due to its nocturnal habits, is the rare Natterjack Toad. Artificial freshwater pools have been dug to encourage this protected creature to breed. As you explore this fascinating area, please be careful to keep to the marked footpaths, as the erosion of the dunes is caused as much by the trampling of feet as by the natural forces of wind and waves.

The name **Liverpool** immediately makes you think of Ferries across the Mersey, the Fab Four, Red Rum, Shirley Valentine and two world famous football teams, but there is much more to this amazing city. In the 19th century, the Port of Liverpool was the gateway to a new world with thousands of British and European emigrants making their way across the atlantic to start a new life in America. Today the historic waterfront with its 1,000 Listed Buildings - including **Albert Dock**, Britain's biggest and most popular heritage attraction - is as busy as ever, for this is a city which, like Manchester, is discovering itself as a major northern tourist centre.

If you are exploring the centre of Liverpool look out for a magnificent building tucked away off Church Street on School Lane in the form of the **Bluecoat Chambers**. This is a superb example of Queen Anne architecture and was built originally as the Bluecoat School. The building occupies three sides of a cobbled courtyard and is today used for a variety of cultural purposes.To the rear is the Bluecoat Gallery which displays the work of many local artists and craftspeople and is a great place to pick up a gift or souvenir. A short walk from here will take you to Matthew Street site of the **Cavern club**, immortalised by the Beatles, and where there are some very good places to eat and drink. Very trendy are The Armadillo tea rooms. Very basic, but super food and always lively. There is a good italian round the corner if you fancy something different.

If you have been to the Albert Dock then you will have already found plenty of places to eat and drink but in the city centre there are still more to choose from.

Prince among Pubs has to be the **Philharmonic**, virtually opposite the concert hall of the same name on Hope Street which is the road that runs between the two cathedrals. The splendid wrought iron gates are a clue to the opulence of the interior which is a riot of stained glass and wood panelling. Parties of tourists are frequently ushered in to see the brass and marble fittings in the Gentleman's toilets, so do be careful!

Liverpool's heyday as a port brought many cultures to the city along with their own types of cooking, and the city is very well served with ethnic restaurants. For Greek try **The Kebab House** around the corner from the Philharmonic, on Hardman Street, or further down the hill on the corner of Leece Street is the wonderful Zorbas. We recommend the Greek banquet or Mezedes. Well recommended. Bookings on 051 709 0190.

Opposite the restaurant at the top of Bold Street is an interesting church called St Lukes. The church was bombed during the war which destroyed all but the shell of the building which stands today as a memorial.

Past the church heading towards the Anglican cathedral there is a good Chinese restaurant on the corner of Duke Street. The **Yuet Ben** has been here for many years and specialises in Peking style cooking.The ribs and duck are first class.

Many of the great merchant warehouses, banks and trading houses of this once mighty port survive along broad streets to give Liverpool a sense of grandeur which lives on. Behind the warehouses and newly pedestrianised areas run narrow streets and alleyways,

Anglican Cathedral

some with old inns and restaurants which were once the haunt of mariners. Since the 1960s, these have been linked to the names of four young men who gave the city a new fame - the Beatles, whose music and 'Mersey Beat' in the Cavern Club became known worldwide. You can now take a daily Beatles Magical History Tour to visit the places that influenced their music, such as Penny Lane and Strawberry Fields - details are available from the Liverpool Information Centre on 051 709 3631.

Liverpool is also a great cultural centre today. The Royal Liverpool Philharmonic Orchestra has an international reputation and is based in the Philharmonic Hall in Hope Street. The Liverpool Playhouse in Williamson Square is Britain's oldest repertory theatre, and the Everyman Theatre and Empire also have an outstanding reputation. If you do decide to go to a show at the Empire Theatre, the Bistro there is highly recommended. The **Walker Art Gallery** has a splendid collection of Great Masters from early Flemish painters to the 20th century, including fine Rembrandts and Cézannes, while the **Northern Tate Gallery** at Albert Dock houses one of the most impressive collections of contemporary art outside London. Albert Dock is also home to the Merseyside Maritime Museum where, among other fascinating exhibits, there is the reconstructed interior of a 19th century emigrants' ship which gives an impression of what it was like for so many people seeking a new life across the Atlantic.

Leaving the city, by keeping the Anglican Cathedral on your left, you will soon be heading towards **Speke Hall**. If you are looking for a place to eat or stay outside the centre yet convenient for both the airport and the town centre you might consider stopping in the Sefton Park/Lark Lane area ,which is off the main A562 Aigburth Road.

Sefton Park was at one time The place to live in Liverpool, and all around the perimeter are houses which were once the homes of the mega rich merchants of the city. Most are, alas, now divided into flats and a couple now serve as hotels, such are their size. The park itself is still a wonderful facility for all to enjoy and is best explored on foot. If you have worked up an appetite you should head for Lark Lane which runs off the park. This victorian suburb has a slightly bohemian air about it and is home to a number of interesting pubs and eateries, the renaissance of this backwater being led many years ago by the local landmark of **Keith's Wine Bar**. Recently extended it still serves excellent food at reasonable prices and has a very good wine list.

Another popular haunt is the **Que Pasa** which serves, surprise surprise, Mexican food, while at the other end of the street is a place we have featured in previous editions, called **L'Allouette**.

Out of the park heading towards the airport there is a turning to the right down Jericho Lane which will take you to the waterfront and Otterspool park. Here there is a marvellous waterside promenade and park, which adjoins the site of the Garden festival which Liverpool hosted some years ago.

Further along the main road again this time on the left as you head out of town is a turning which has a discreet sign pointing you to the Grange Hotel, a good choice as a place to stay. Quiet and comfortable. Reservations on 051 427 2950.

Travelling along the A561 towards the southern end of the Mersey estuary, you will come to Speke, a name probably familiar because of its airport. However, it is also the home of **Speke Hall**, a beautiful half-timbered Elizabethan manor house whose grounds have a wealth of interesting features for the whole family to explore. When visiting the Hall you can discover the secrets behind the eavesdrop chamber, or find out what life was like below stairs in the servants' hall and kitchen. You may even bump into the tapestry ghost on your travels. The oldest parts of Speke Hall were built nearly 500 years ago by the Norris family. Over succeeding generations, the building developed around a cobbled courtyard which is dominated by two yew trees, known locally as Adam and Eve.

The Great Hall dates back to Tudor times, but has considerably altered over the years. The house as we see it today owes much to the refurbishments carried out in Victorian times, with many of the smaller panelled rooms containing fine furnishings from the arts and crafts movement, designed by William Morris. Outside, there are superb grounds and gardens. The moat which surrounded the house in the 17th century has now been drained and forms a feature of the grounds, which include a Victorian Rose Garden, a Croquet lawn, ancient woodland and the raised walk, which offers fine views across the Mersey.

To make a visit even more enjoyable, the National Trust has an on-site tea room, serving light lunches with home baking, teas and ices, and a shop where you can purchase books, stationery, souvenirs and gifts. For the disabled, much of the house, garden, woodland walk, and tea room is accessible; lavatories have been adapted to facilitate wheelchairs, and free use of a wheelchair is also available. Special events are arranged throughout the year and include music, drama and walks. Situated on the Northern bank of the Mersey, Speke Hall is just six miles east of Liverpool city centre and only thirty minutes from Chester.

Speke Hall, The Walk, Liverpool Tel: 051 427 7231
Fax: 051 427 9860

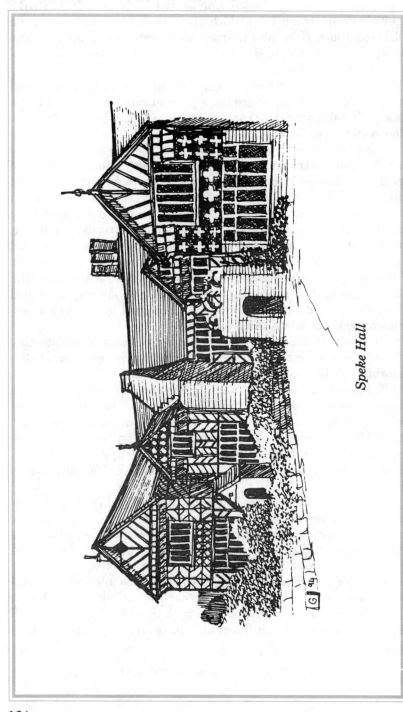

Speke Hall

WEST LANCASHIRE AND MERSEYSIDE

Outside of Liverpool, in the area to the east of the city, there are lots of interesting places to visit. In the town of **St. Helens**, there is the fascinating **Pilkington Glass Museum**, which traces the story of glass making. At **Prescott**, there is the equally interesting **Prescott Museum of Clock and Watchmaking.**

At nearby **Knowsley**, there is something for all the family at **Knowsley Safari Park**. At one price per car, including all passengers, you can drive through the 450 acres of rolling countryside where many of the world's wildest animals roam free. You could see the largest herd of African elephants in Europe, lions, tigers, baboons, buffalo, rhion, zebra, camels and many more. In addition there is a pets corner for the children, sealion shows, reptile house, a miniature railway and an amusement park. The Park is open daily from March to October and visitors should arrive no later than 4pm.

For those who want a day out that is that little bit more exciting, then why not have a day at the races. There are two racecourses here. **Aintree**, home of the world's greatest steeplechase, the Grand National, hosts 2 race meetings each year - the National Festival in early April and the Bechers meeting in mid-November. **Haydock Park Racecourse** offers 28 race days per year covering both the Flat and National Hunt calendars.

Leaving Merseyside behind us, the next chapter takes us across to the Wirral and on to the western half of Cheshire.

St George's Hall, Liverpool

The Wirral and West Cheshire

Church Farm, Bidston Village, Wirral

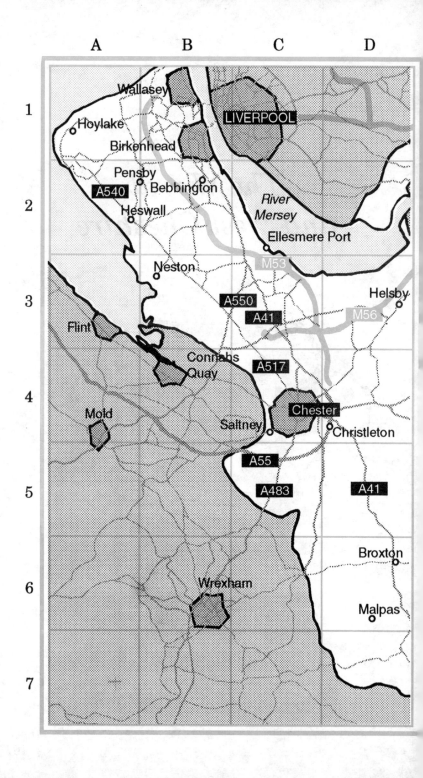

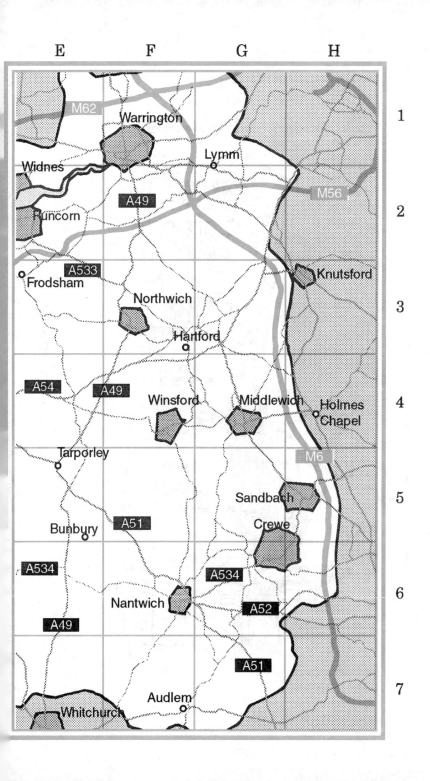

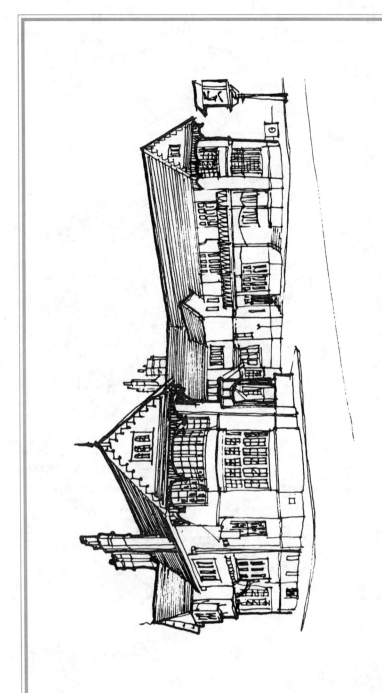

The Bridge Inn, Port Sunlight

The Wirral and West Cheshire

For a real Merseyside experience, you have to take a Ferry 'Cross the Mersey. The services today continue in the tradition of Mersey river crossings that began in 1207. These powerful little vessels, strong enough to withstand the Mersey tides, have been refurbished in traditional style and provide a miniature cruise between Pier Head at Liverpool, **Seacombe** and **Woodside** in Birkenhead. The views from the ferry back down the estuary to the famous Liverpool waterfront, are truly memorable.

The Wirral is also readily accessible by road with a comprehensive motorway network giving access from Liverpool via one of the two road tunnels, or from Cheshire via the M53. Alternatively Merseyrail, the local rail network, serves the northern part of the Wirral extremely efficiently, with frequent services to Chester, Liverpool and towns across the peninsula.

The Wirral describes itself, with good reason, as the Leisure Peninsula. Though the once great industry of shipbuilding at Birkenhead has declined, much of the area has undergone a change, not only with the restoration and smartening up of ferry terminii, but with the creation of attractive walkways along the seafront. If elegant Hamilton Square no longer contains the smart town houses of sea captains, Birkenhead Priory, the chapter house of a Benedictine monastery established in 1150 AD, now a church, has changed little and contains a Heritage Centre and Museum.

Birkenhead Park to the east of the town centre is a remarkable example of an early Victorian urban park, with lake, rockery, lawns, and formal gardens, which interestingly enough became the model for an even more famous park - Central Park in New York.

Near **Birkenhead** town centre on East Float Dock Road you will find a pair of historic warships, now museums. Both the frigate HMS Plymouth and submarine HMS Onyx served during the Falklands conflict and are now preserved so you can discover for yourselves what life is like aboard a ship of the Royal Navy. Open from 10am daily you can get further details on 051 650 1573.

If you take the train from Liverpool Lime Street's Merseyrail Underground station to **West Kirby**, within a few minutes walk of the station you can be on the Wirral Way. This is a 12 mile long walkway along the old West Kirby - Hooton railway line, leading into Wirral Country Park. At **Thurstaton** some three miles along the line and just off the A540, there is a car park and an excellent Countryside Centre close by. Here you'll find a choice of walks and trails along the coast. Continuing along the railway to **Neston** and **Hooton** via Hadlow Road you'll discover a perfectly restored railway station without any trains.

Wirral is full of the most fascinating villages to explore, among them **Bidston** which has a hilltop observatory and windmill close by, and Oxton, a conservation area, which is noted for fine views.

Port Sunlight Heritage Centre, 95 Greendale Road, Port Sunlight
Tel: 051 644 6466

Most fascinating of all perhaps, though relatively modern, is **Port Sunlight** Village. This is a model garden village, founded in 1888 by William Hesketh Lever to house his soap factory workers. It was named after his most famous product, Sunlight Soap. The village is officially rated as a Conservation Area. In March of 1888, Mrs Lever cut the first sod of Port Sunlight, and thus helped to lay the foundations of a village which was to be appreciated by many generations to come. It was the aim of her husband, who later became the first Viscount Leverhulme, to provide for his workers 'a new Arcadia, ventilated and drained on the most scientific principles'. He took great pleasure in helping to plan this most picturesque garden village, and he employed nearly 30 different architects to create its unique style.

Port Sunlight is now a conservation area, still within its original boundaries. The history of this village and its community is explored in **Port Sunlight Heritage Centre**, where there is a scale model of

Hadlow Road Station, on the Wirral Way

Bidston Windmill

the village and of a Victorian Port, Sunlight House, the original plans for the buildings, and displays of period advertising and soap packaging. The Village Trail shows you the Village's attractions, including the Lady Lever Art Gallery, which contains Lord Leverhulme's world famous collections of pre-Raphaelite paintings and Wedgwood. Pre-booked guided tours of the Village are available from the Heritage Centre for parties and schools, and a Village Trail leaflet enables visitors to find their way around.

If you are looking for somewhere different to eat, then why not try the restaurant which is situated in the basement of the Lady Lever Art Gallery (pre-booking needed for large groups). It offers fine foods, a wonderful setting, and fascinating and beautiful treasures to appreciate.

Just off the busy A41 road from Birkenhead, it is worth a detour to discover the little village of **Eastham**, mentioned in the Domesday book, and which has some very interesting buildings, including the local church which is reputed to have the oldest yew tree in England in its grounds. There is a local pub, and a park which is right on the river Mersey. Sometimes from the park, you are rewarded with wonderful views of the large tankers which glide upriver to the refinery at **Stanlow**. On Ferry Road in the middle of the village is a marvellous find for those of you who like to browse around antique shops, in the form of **Eastham Antiques**. Peter and Gill Lightfoot converted a barn in the rear garden of their cottage and opened the business some 20 years ago. They carry a selection of furniture and bric-a-brac and this is also a good place to call if you are in the market for a genuine brass and iron bed. Open most days and at weekends, Eastham Antiques are well worth a visit.

Eastham Antiques, Ferry Road, Eastham, Wirral Tel: 051 327 5563

Willaston-in-Wirral is another charming village which has a

174

windmill, as well as a number of 17th century cottages and a village green.

Situated on Benty Heath Lane, just outside Willaston, you will find an excellent place to stay at **Raby House Hotel,** an impressive red brick building originally built in 1867 as a private house for the Johnson family of the Liverpool Shipping Line. Very much a family-run hotel, Raby House successfully combines a high standard of accommodation and service with a friendly, relaxed atmosphere, making it an ideal holiday or touring base. The twelve guest rooms are tastefully decorated and equipped for maximum comfort. When it comes to dining, you can opt for one of the very reasonably priced bar meals, or choose from the extensive à la carte menu in the Raby House Restaurant. All meals are freshly prepared to order ensuring complete satisfaction.

Raby House Hotel, Benty Heath Lane, Willaston-in-Wirral, Cheshire Tel: 051 327 1900

While you are in this part of Wirral, it is well worth spending a day out at The Boat Museum in **Ellesmere Port,** a living museum with a unique collection of boats, exhibitions, engines and much more. Home to the world's largest collection of traditional canal boats, visitors can step aboard into some of the cabins and discover how canal people managed to live and raise families in a home no bigger than the hallway of a modern house. Situated in an historic dock complex where the Shropshire Union and Manchester Ship Canals meet, during the summer months visitors can enjoy leisurely boat trips and experience the flavour of a bygone age.

To the east of Ellesmere Port, just off the M56 lies the tiny village of **Preston Brook** where, for well over 100 years, the **Red Lion Hotel** has been providing visitors and locals with welcome refreshment and first class accommodation. Awarded a Two Crowns rating, this attractive hotel makes a popular stopping-off point for canal travellers and offers a fine selection of well-kept ales and a varied menu of homecooked fayre, including a special selection for children. Owned and personally run by Paul Butler the Red Lion's inviting exterior is matched by the cosy, well-furnished interior and for those seeking overnight accommodation there are seven well-equipped, en-suite guest rooms. There is ample off-road parking and on fine summer days, you can enjoy your drink and meal outside.

Red Lion Hotel, Chester Road, Preston Brook, Runcorn
Tel: 0928 701174

Within easy reach from here, Norton Priory is always a delightful and intriguing place for a family visit, whatever the weather. Despite being situated close to Junction 11 of the M56, it lies in a peaceful oasis just outside **Runcorn**, with 16 acres of beautiful woodland gardens in which to wander and enjoy a picnic.

The Augustinian Priory was built as the prosperous abode for 12 canons in 1134. It was transformed into a Tudor and then a Georgian mansion before it was abandoned in 1921. Daily life for the canons was strictly disciplined and a typical day would consist of prayer, worship and work duties, with some time set aside for relaxation according to the rule of St Augustine. The main activity would be worship, so the day was almost wholly taken up with attending the church services. The canons were known as 'Black Canons' because their outer garment was a cape of black woollen cloth, worn over a white linen surplice. Life was not as spartan for them as one would imagine because they ate two meals a day in the refectory or dining room. We know they were allowed to eat meat because when excavations were carried out, many bones of animals were found. As well as a staple diet, beer was the drink that accompanied their meals.

Day-to-day life in 12th century Cheshire is reflected through the

Ellesmere Port Boat Museum

exhibitions which have been created in the prize winning Museum. Age old crafts and art forms such as tile making and sculpture are revived and celebrated in workshops and demonstrations which are held periodically throughout the year. Just a short walk away is Cheshire's best kept secret - the Walled Garden, which received a special prize in the 1990 Britain in Bloom competition.

In nearby **Widnes** you will find the **Hillcrest Hotel** which, from its humble beginnings 25 years ago as a five bedroomed house providing bed and breakfast for visitors to the area, is now one of the North West's premier hotels, providing excellence in every department. All of the 51 guest rooms are en-suite and equipped for maximum comfort and yet despite its size, this Four Crowns rated hotel still retains the very friendly, personal atmosphere of its early days. Harold and Sue Nelson are welcoming and experienced hosts whose priority is clearly guest comfort and satisfaction. From the nautically themed Nelson's Bar to the Palms Restaurant with its extensive and imaginative à la carte menu, everything about Hillcrest Hotel assures you of a relaxing and enjoyable stay.

Hillcrest Hotel, Cronton Lane, Widnes Tel: 051 424 1616
Fax: 051 495 1348

Also in Widnes you will find **Catalyst**, the Museum of the Chemical Industry. This fascinating museum is located close to the River Mersey and the Runcorn-Widnes Bridge, and is open daily except Mondays. This award-winning Museum, which claims to be a world first, explores various aspects of one of Cheshire's greatest industries, with an emphasis on 'hands-on' scientific exploration for the whole family. There is also a programme of special events throughout the year.

North east of Widnes, **Warrington** is North Cheshire's largest town and the main focus for industrial development in the region. It lies both on an important bridging point of the River Mersey, midway between the huge conurbations and ports of Manchester and Liverpool, and on a nodal point of communications close to where the M6, M62 and M56 motorways intersect and where the electrified West Coast Main Line railway links London and Scotland. Not for nothing does Warrington, with its excellent communications, claim to enjoy Britain's most central location.

In past years Warrington was most famous for its heavy industry, including the manufacture of chemicals and the production of steel rope and wire for industry. Today the town is also an important centre for brewing, soap manufacture and scientific research, but it still has several fine Georgian and Victorian buildings around the town centre and a pleasant central shopping centre around Horsemarket Street. The Town Hall is a former country house built in 1750 for Lord Winmarleigh, before being acquired with its park by the Council in 1872. Some of the windows are framed in copper and the magnificent cast iron gates, which are 25 feet high and 54 feet broad, were given to the town in 1893.

Holly Lodge Hotel, 10 Froghall Lane, Warrington Tel: 0925 36273

On Froghall Lane in Warrington, just a two minute walk from the town centre and railway station, you will find a very comfortable place to stay at the **Holly Lodge Hotel**, home of Sandra and Don Wooden. Built in 1860, the hotel is full of character, retaining many period features, and in the five years since they have been here, Sandra and Don have turned it into relaxed and welcoming establishment. The hotel has its own private car park and there are eleven tastefully decorated guest rooms, five with en-suite facilities and each morning you can enjoy a substantial breakfast to set you up for the day. Although there are no evening meals available, Holly Lodge is licensed and its close proximity to the town centre puts many restaurants within easy reach.

Another good reason for visiting Warrington is its excellent Museum and Art Gallery in Bold Street, one of the earliest Municipal Museums in the country, dating from 1857, and a real Aladdin's Cave in the very best Victorian tradition. The museum collection dates from 1848 and contains everything from shrunken heads, a unique china teapot collection, a scold's bridle, Egyptian mummys, a rare Roman actor's mask and other Roman artefacts discovered in nearby Wilderspool. There are some fine paintings as well, most of which are Victorian watercolours and oils, but also a rare Vanous still life.

On Station road in Latchford, just east of Warrington, you would be well advised to call in at **Cantilever Garden Centre**, one of four family-run businesses which form the group "Garden Centres of Cheshire". As with the other three members of the group, quality is the highest priority here and there is a large selection of plants and shrubs available all year round. Originally a station yard, this was the original Centre and has been here for 25 years, enjoying a unique position overlooking the Manchester Ship Canal. The centre has a well deserved reputation for the service and high standards it offers its many customers and in addition to selling plants, offers a wide choice of garden furniture, equipment and accessories to cater to your every need. Having made your purchases, you can complete your visit by savouring the homemade snacks available in the Centre's well-run coffee shop.

Cantilever Garden Centre, Station Road, Latchford, Warrington
Tel: 0925 35799

Just yards off the main A57 at **Glazebrook**, you will discover a real gem at **Mount Pleasant Craft Centre**. Housed within old converted barns, there is something here to appeal to the whole family. A homely, friendly atmosphere is immediately apparent and this

180

Baby Rhino, Chester Zoo

wonderful Centre houses an abundance of quality crafts, beginning on the ground floor in the craft shop with its rich display of pottery, jewellery, walking sticks, mobiles and much more besides. The adjoining card boutique provides cards of every description to suit any occasion and between these two areas is the needlework stable which supplies everything the needlework enthusiast could possibly need. A passage leads from here to Conservatory Interiors which houses a stunning display of cane and wicker furniture. After all this, it must be time for refreshment and the tea and coffee shop with its welcoming log fires caters for everything, from light snacks to full meals. From here it's upstairs to an area offering embroidery classes and then through into the attractive dried flower display. As its name suggests,'Something for Grandma to Buy' is a corner full of suitable gifts for the grandchildren. Finally, take a look around the Fashion Loft before calling in at the Farmhouse Kitchen with its collection of quality pottery, china and kitchen utensils.

Mount Pleasant Farm Craft Centre, Glazebrook, Near Warrington
Tel: 061 775 2004

Somewhat hidden, but nevertheless ideally situated for both the holiday and business traveller, **The Rhinewood Hotel** can be reached by following the A57, taking the turning onto the B5212 and continuing for about two miles, after which the hotel can be seen on the right hand side. This former Georgian rectory has been sympathetically renovated and extended to create a hotel which, despite its modern appearance, still holds true to traditional values of service and hospitality. Awarded a Three Crowns grading, all thirty en-suite guest rooms are attractively furnished and equipped for maximum comfort. The bar provides a relaxed setting for an aperitif or night-cap which on certain evenings can be enjoyed to the backdrop of live music from the piano. The elegant restaurant offers the discerning guest a
182

choice of both à la carte and table d'hôte menus, with an extensive selection for vegetarians, all accompanied by a choice wine list.

The Rhinewood Hotel, Glazebrook Lane, Glazebrook, Near Warrington Tel: 061 775 5555

Just south of Glazebrook lies Risley Moss Nature Park, over 200 acres of scattered woodland, mossland, ponds and pools. Make time to call in at the visitor centre and climb the Observation Tower with its magnificent views of the Peak District fells nearly 30 miles away. Close by is Birchwood Forest Park, which lies about half a mile from the Birchwood/Warrington intersection of the M62.

Holly Bank Caravan Park, Warburton Bridge Road, Rixton Tel: 061 775 2842

For those who prefer the freedom of a camping holiday, situated 2 miles east of Junction 21 (M6) on the A57 at **Rixton**, in open countryside between Warrington and Manchester, **Holly Bank Caravan Park** makes a super base. There has been a park on this site since

1978 and the current owners Jim and Sheilagh Walsh took over in 1987, having returned after 20 years living in Australia. Probably one of the best caravan parks in Cheshire, Holly Bank carries a well-deserved Four Ticks rating under the ETB quality grading scheme. It is set in nine acres of lovely grounds and can accommodate up to 75 tourers and 10-15 tents. Facilities include a well-stocked shop, hot showers, toilet block, 55 electric hook-ups, a games room, launderette, adventure play area and public telephone. Open all year.

Another delightful village close to Warrington is **Lymm**, also on the Bridgewater Canal, with half-timbered houses, a market cross and village stocks. Lymm developed as an important centre for the fustian cloth trade in the 19th century. Lymm Dam is a large man-made lake in a lovely woodland centre which is linked to surrounding countryside and to the canal towpath by a network of footpaths and bridleways. The Dam is popular for angling and birdwatching.

Stained glass window detail from Daresbury Church, birthplace of Lewis Carroll

184

Please don't forget...
To tell people that you read about them in
The Hidden Places

For lovers of fine food, the **Lymm Bistro** in Bridgewater Street can be found in an attractive 200-year old building and has been run for the past five years by Jo Shenton and Michael Venning. Since opening the Bistro, Jo and Michael have earned themselves an excellent reputation for providing first class food and wines. Michael is the chef, and he has obviously gone to great lengths to ensure that his diners receive only the very best and freshest of produce. Meals are cooked to order and served in the cosy, friendly atmosphere which the Bistro exudes. Michael's speciality is fish, and this can be anything from a simple but exquisite whole Dover Sole, to really exotic and exciting dishes. For example, it is not unknown for Michael to offer amongst his daily specials such unusual dishes as giant Australian Snow Crab, Barracuda Shark, or Parrot Fish. As one can imagine, offering dishes such as these makes the Lymm Bistro very popular, and it is not surprising that diners travel from far and wide to sample such excellent cuisine. Jo and Michael are on hand every evening to look after the personal requirements of their diners. In order to do justice to the menu which Michael has so thoughtfully put together, we feel we must enlarge upon the dishes which are offered.

The Lymm Bistro

Lymm Bistro, 16 Bridgewater Street, Lymm Tel: 0925 75 4852

Blackboard specials are always popular, and a selection of starters

185

may consist of Avocado filled with Smoked Salmon and topped with a tomato vinaigrette, fresh Squid cooked with tomato and red wine, or perhaps plump Frogs Legs sautéed with onions and garlic and flamed in Brandy. The main courses are just as mouthwatering. We particularly liked the sound of fresh Marlin Fish, sautéed with various Shellfish, served in a cream sauce. We were just as impressed with the Wild Boar - a roast saddle of Wild Boar served in a sauce made from its own juices, Juniper Berries and Port. By now we are quite sure that we will have whetted your appetite, and can only conclude by suggesting that prior to visiting, you telephone and reserve your table. As you can imagine, the Lymm Bistro does become extremely busy and with a Table d'hôte menu available during the week as well, represents superb value for money.

Willow Pool Nursery and Garden Centre, Burford Lane, Lymm
Tel: 0925 757827

Another place well worth calling in at while you are in Lymm is **Willow Pool Nursery and Garden Centre**, which is situated off the A56 on the B5159. There has been a nursery on this site for over 50 years and although the roots, as they say, were planted many years ago, Willow Pool has really taken shape in the four years that the present owner, Sonny Brunsveld, a Dutchman, has been here. Management is in the capable hands of James and Jose. Within the nurseries you will find everything you need for your garden and James will happily share his knowledge and expertise with you, offering a wealth of useful advice. In addition to a full range of plants and garden supplies, an added attraction is the lovely large wooded area in which you can wander at your leisure, with a pond which is home to a wide variety of wildfowl.

Travelling out of Lymm on the B5160 Lymm road towards Altrincham, you will discover **Dunham Massey Hall**, one of Cheshire's most outstanding National Trust properties. It was built in 1732 for George Booth, the 2nd Earl of Warrington, who commissioned the little known architect, John Norris who perceived the idea of encasing an earlier Tudor building. The 2nd Earl was also responsible for laying out the park, and purchasing the collection of furnishings and Huguenot silver. The house and estate subsequently became the principal home to the 9th Earl of Stamford in 1905. It was he who commissioned another architect by the name of Compton Hall to undertake the alterations to the south front of the house, which we see today.

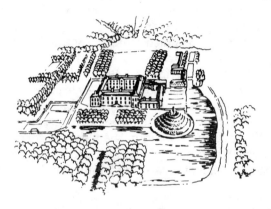

Dunham Massey Hall, Altrincham, Cheshire Tel: 061 941 1025

The interior of the house and its refurbishment owes much to the sensitivity of Percy Macquoid, who handled the redecoration of the state rooms. He is acknowledged as being one of the finest and most distinguished furniture historians. The house was bequeathed to the National Trust in 1976 by Roger the 10th Earl of Stamford. Many of the paintings, prints and photographs are of the prominent Booth and Grey families, who through their association with Dunham Massey have left their mark for future generations to appreciate.

As visitors wander through the house, they can catch a glimpse of personal possessions such as documents and books which formerly belonged to members of the Booth and Grey families. One cannot fail to be impressed by the craftsmanship, richness and elegance of such a magnificent house with such fine furnishings.

In sympathy with the house, the garden is being restored by the Trust, and broadly speaking is in the character of the late-Victorian Pleasure Ground. The Trust has managed to retain modified parts of the Edwardian scheme such as the parterre, and the notable remnants of earlier schemes. Organised events such as midsummer music evenings are staged throughout the year. Visitors are encouraged to

187

visit the licensed restaurant for refreshments and the National Trust shop for souvenirs.

Just west of Lymm lies the village of **Grappenhall**, a village of Cheshire thatched cottages, with its church standing by the banks of the Bridgewater Canal. If you look carefully above the west window of the church tower, you'll find the carved figure of a cat with a grin. This is thought to have been the original Cheshire Cat which featured in Lewis Carroll's 'Alice in Wonderland', and which has become a symbol of the County of Cheshire.

On the corner of Victoria Road and the A50 Knutsford Road, you will find an excellent holiday base at the **Kenilworth Hotel**. Awarded a Three Crowns Commended grading by the English Tourist Board, AA and RAC Acclaimed, this turn of the century building has been completely refurbished and extended over the past eight years by current owners, the Strickland family, who have turned it into a very homely, welcoming establishment. A warm, friendly atmosphere is immediately apparent and it is clear that guests' needs are of paramount importance. All of the seventeen guest rooms are en-suite and attractively furnished and in the pleasant surroundings of the restaurant you can choose from an excellent à la carte menu, freshly prepared to very high standards by family member, Roberto.

Kenilworth Hotel, 2 Victoria Road, Grappenhall Tel: 0925 262323

East of here on the A50 is **High Legh** and this is definitely the place to visit if you are a keen gardener. **High Legh Garden Centre** was opened in 1987 and is truly a garden centre of excellence. With its huge range of plants, shrubs, tools and accessories, it is a mecca for any gardening enthusiast. A large car park gives immediate access to the many trees and shrubs on display. Huge polytunnels have been erected to ensure that all plant material goes on sale, and remains, in tip top condition. The primary aim of High Legh Garden Centre is that quality and service remain at all times a top priority. A wide selection of top quality outdoor plants are on view, and undercover areas protect the more vulnerable of species. There is a large range of speciality house plants which include Bonsai, Cacti and Airplants, as well as an Aquatics Centre with numerous aquaria, fish, plants and other accessories.

One of the highlights of the Centre is the well-established gift shop which prides itself on the constantly changing selection of gifts. Many new and original items are to be found here and ideas range from china, glassware, ornaments and prints, to toiletries, men's gifts, confectionery, stationery, toys, books, pet supplies, fireworks and all items relating to the Christmas season. The Centre also supplies a top range of greenhouses, conservatories and garden furniture. Their range of French furniture was recently awarded the 'Best Display' in the North West. There are also many demonstrations and events held during the year, but particularly around Christmas time, when the children's Grotto is always original and popular. Also on site is a superb fern-filled Café which provides a welcome opportunity to enjoy a full meal or a snack. Children are well catered for and there is a very safe and well-equipped play area set aside for them.

High Legh Garden Centre, High Legh, Near Knutsford
Tel: 0925 756991

To the west, you will find the charming village of **Appleton Thorn** where every year the locals celebrate 'Bauming' the thorn. This unique custom owes its origin to a Norman knight, Adam de Dutton, who according to tradition returned in the 12th century from the Crusades with a cutting from the Glasonbury Thorn to plant at Appleton as a thanksgiving for his safe return. The present tree outside the church was planted in 1967 and is meant to be a direct descendant of the original. The ceremony takes place on the third

Saturday in June, when young children decorate the tree and sing the 'Bauming song', written by the 19th century Cheshire Poet, R.E Egerton-Warburton.

Arley Hall and Gardens, Arley, Near Northwich Tel: 0565 777353

Arley Hall lies about three miles south-east of Appleton Thorn. The Arley estate is one of the few remaining to have survived in Cheshire as a family home with resident owners still living on the estate. The house and gardens have been owned by the family of the Hon. Michael Flower and Mrs. Flower for more than 500 years. Arley is an agricultural estate deep in the North Cheshire countryside, yet it is only five miles from the M6 and M56. The Hall, which is set in 12 acres of one of the finest gardens in England, contains excellent examples of panelling, plasterwork, furniture and family portraits.

Also on the estate is a chapel, gift shop, garden nursery selling plants, a tea room and a picture gallery with paintings by local artists. The gardens, which have won several awards over the years, offer great variety and interest and can be explored with the use of a guide book written by Lady Ashbrook. The task of writing the booklet was one for which she was uniquely qualified, having known the gardens intimately all her life. The guide describes something of the historical background of the gardens and is designed to lead the visitor round in a logical sequence. Also of interest is the fact that in the past, each succeeding generation of Lady Ashbrook's family has contributed to the development of the gardens. The present owners, Mr. and Mrs. Flower, have followed tradition by reinstating the Grove - an area of everchanging colour - and creating a woodland walk near the chapel which has become a great source of enjoyment to visitors. The old estate yard is set aside for the workshops of local craftsmen making custom-built furniture.

Stockley Farm on the estate welcomes visitors to the award-winning modern working dairy farm which is of particular interest to families. A tractor and trailer transports visitors to the farm where they can see cows being milked, play with and feed the animals and enjoy the milk bar, straw bounce and shop.

We are certain that readers will thoroughly enjoy visiting this delightful Hall and Gardens and therefore recommend telephoning for more information, the number is 0565 777353.

Not far from here is **Great Budworth**, with its charming red brick and timber framed cottages with twisted chimneys, all clustered round a green hill and the handsome parish church of St Mary and All Siants. Great Budworth was once the largest ecclesiastical parish in Cheshire, encompassing 35 individual townships, most of which are now independent. The church itself was built between the 14th and 15th centuries and is famous for its crowd of quaint carvings and odd faces that peer out at unexpected corners: some with staring eyes, others with their tongues poking out at the unwary visitor. Look for a man tired of too many sermons near the pulpit; under the roof of the nave you'll find a man with a serpent, another trying to turn a somersault, and a minstrel plays his bagpipes. The famous 17th century historian, Sir Peter Leycester is buried in the Lady Chapel and in the Warburton Chapel there is a fine carved Tudor ceiling and 13th century oak stalls - the oldest in Cheshire.

Wincham Wharf, 216/220 Manchester Road, Lostock Gralam, Northwich Tel: 0606 48581

To the south, **Wincham Wharf** is a working boatyard on the banks of the Trent and Mersey Canal, situated at **Lostock Gralam**, just outside Northwich. Opened in 1777, the canal provided a link between the industrial midlands and the Mersey Basin and it was at Wincham Wharf that goods were received and the horses were changed, fed and farriered. Today, Wincham Wharf is home to a super bar and restau-

Sundial at Great Budworth Church

rant run by Margaret and Richard Tallis. Full of character, with exposed beams and brickwork, the bar offers a fine selection of well-kept ale accompanied by tasty bar snacks. Upstairs, the cosy 50-seater restaurant oozes style and class and offers an extensive menu of excellent and reasonably priced homecooked fayre to appeal to every palate, making this one place not to be missed.

If you enjoy strolling around garden centres and nurseries, then we recommend a visit to **Ascol Drive Nursery**. Situated just off the A556 Altrincham to Chester road, take the turning opposite the sign for Northwich. Jacqueline and Dinkie Bristow who own the nursery have been here for just five years and in that time they have put in an incredible amount of work. Considering the way in which the nursery is laid out and organised, it is almost impossible to believe that they have been here for such a short time. Besides the visual items grown and sold in nurseries, they also specialise in hanging baskets and Christmas wreaths. Conifers are grown from rooted cuttings and carefully tended. Prices are extremely reasonable, whether you purchase flowers, shrubs, bedding plants or seeds. Nothing is too much trouble for the Bristow family and they will happily impart their expertise to customers. The site covers four acres and allows visitors to browse around at leisure. You may like to purchase one of their magnificent hanging baskets while you are here.

Did You Know...

There is a full list of

Tourist Information Centres

at the back of the book?

Ascol Drive Nursery, Ascol Drive, Plumley, Near Northwich
Tel: 0606 47694

Just north of here lies **Pickmere**, a delightful village commanding superb views of the Cheshire Plain from the Dee Estuary to the Pennine foothills. Not only is it ideally situated for exploring Cheshire's peaks, plains, parks and waterways, but it is readily accessible, being close to Manchester Airport and only two miles from junction 19 of the M6 motorway. This makes it an ideal stopover point for both northbound and southbound travellers. Chester, Manchester and Liverpool can all be reached within 40 minutes. Leisure activities in the area include golf, riding and watersports.

Situated just a few hundred yards from the famous Pickmere Lake and adjacent to Pickmere Caravan Park is **The Elms**. Built in 1909 it was originally an alehouse on the old Bradbury estate and is now a free house run by Ken and Sue Moore. There is good off-road parking here and a stylish patio area is ideal for sitting out on warm days and in the Summer is frequently used for barbeques. Inside, The Elms is beautifully decorated and the roaring log fire enhances the warm, friendly atmosphere. Children, pets and the disabled are all welcomed and catered for. Traditional bar snacks are available with daily specials.

The Elms, Park Lane, Pickmere Tel:0565 733395

If you are looking for a place to stay, then not far from here, situated in the heart of the Cheshire countryside at **Weaverham**, **The Oaklands** is an elegant country hotel run by the highly experienced Southerton family. Providing a secluded and relaxing holiday base, the hotel stands within six and a half acres of beautifully landscaped grounds and exudes an air of grandeur. Dating back to the 17th century, the history and character of this splendid hotel are reflected in each of the tastefully furnished rooms, enhanced by wood panelled walls and open fireplaces. All eleven guest rooms are en-suite and equipped for maximum comfort and before dinner you can enjoy an aperitif in the welcoming atmosphere of The Oaklands Bar which has an excellent range of well-kept ale. The delightful conservatory restaurant provides the perfect setting in which to savour the excellent cuisine on the à la carte menu and afterwards you can retire to the comfort of the main lounge with a night-cap.

The nearby town of **Northwich** lies on the confluence of the Rivers

Weaver and Dane. Its name derives from 'wych', meaning salt town. Salt has been extracted from Cheshire since before Roman times. In 1670 rock salt was discovered in nearby Marston, and Northwich developed as a major salt producer. In the 19th century, Brunner and Mond set up their salt works at **Winnington** to manufacture alkali products based on brine.

The Oaklands, Millington Lane, Gorstage, Weaverham
Tel: 0606 853249 Fax: 0606 852419

Extensive pumping of brine has, however, caused subsidence and large holes often used to appear, even swallowing up buildings. Salt extraction is now carefully controlled, but you can still see flooded areas, or flashes, around the town and on Witton Street, the White Lion Inn has sunk an entire storey! The subsidence led to the design of a new type of timber framed building in the area which can be jacked up as required.

Situated in the Northwich Workhouse building on London Road is Britain's only Salt Museum. With its unique collection of traditional working tools and lively displays which include working models and videos, the Salt Museum tells the fascinating story of Cheshire's oldest industry. Not only can ancient remains such as Roman evaporating pans and medieval salt rakes be seen, but there is much to remind visitors of the vital part that salt plays in the modern chemical industry.

Conveniently situated on Middlewich Road, just half a mile from the picturesque town centre of Northwich and only five minutes drive from junction 19 of the M6, **Park Dale Guest House** makes an ideal touring base from which to explore the many attractions of Cheshire. Bought some six years ago as a derelict building, owners Carl and Rose have developed this into a charming place to stay, with six spacious and attractively furnished guest rooms, three of which are en-suite. The lovely breakfast/dining room provides the perfect setting in which to savour Rose's excellent cooking. In addition to a substantial breakfast each morning, she will happily provide you with a packed lunch to take out with you and a homecooked evening meal upon your return if required.

Park Dale Guest House, 140 Middlewich Road, Rudheath, Northwich Tel: 0606 45228

Situated on Winnington Lane in Northwich, you will discover **Weaver Vale Garden Centre**, one of four family-run businesses that come under the title of "Garden Centres of Cheshire". This is the most recent addition to the group and as well as providing a wide and varied selection of plants and shrubs, also has its own machinery department complete with fully equipped workshop where customers are welcome to visit.

Weaver Vale Garden Centre, Winnington Lane, Northwich Tel: 0606 79965

The Centre is set within beautiful lawned grounds and has everything you could need for the garden from Garden Furniture and Barbeques to ponds and liners and all the relevant accessories, from ornamental garden pots to fencing, walling and paving. The Centre's large gift shop sells numerous items including attractive dried flowers, preserves, chocolates and books, while in the coffee shop you can enjoy tasty cakes, snacks and meals.

The tiny hamlet of **Acton Bridge** can be reached off the old A49 at Weaverham and it is here on Hilltop Road that you will find **The Maypole Inn**. This welcoming hostelry has been providing passing visitors and locals with refreshment for hundreds of years and current proprietors Keith and Brenda Morris continue to provide the friendly hospitality which has made this inn so popular. Outside there is a large car park and a children's play area whilst the interior is full of character, with a vast open fireplace, bygone memorabilia and lovely beamed ceilings enhancing a warm cosy atmosphere. Keith and Brenda pride themselves on serving well-kept ale and a wide selection of tasty, homecooked fayre, making this an ideal venue for a family lunch.

The Maypole Inn, Hilltop Road, Acton Bridge Tel: 0606 853114

For visitors to the area looking for a place to stay, just two and a half miles south of junction 10 off the M56, **Tall Trees Lodge** makes an ideal base from which to explore the surrounding Cheshire countryside. Opened in October 1992 by owners Denise and Paul Garnett, the modern exterior of this hotel belies the warm, friendly atmosphere within which makes this far and above the run of the mill lodge. The twenty en-suite guest rooms are attractively furnished and equipped to a high standard for maximum comfort and the newly opened bar provides the perfect setting in which to relax with a quiet drink and light snack. With the Little Chef situated next door, you have ready

197

access to full meals throughout the day and travelling out a little way, you will find yourself within easy reach of many charming country pubs serving excellent food to suit all tastes.

Tall Trees Lodge, Tarporley Road, Lower Whitley, Near Warrington Tel: 0928 790824 Fax: 0928 791330

To the west of Northwich lies the village of **Kingsley**, the site of Kingsley Mill which has stood for approximately 300 years. Originally there was a waterwheel attached to the mill, but this was dismantled just over 25 years ago. The mill still produces and manufactures animal feeds, as well as being home to the Country Clothing Riding Equipment retailers. This has been developed over the past seven years and sells everything that a horse rider may require.

Forest Hills Hotel, Overton Hill, Frodsham Tel: 0928 735255 Fax: 0928 735517

Not far from here, in the heart of the rolling Cheshire countryside at Overton Hill and yet less than five minutes drive from the M56,

Forest Hills Hotel near Frodsham provides a luxurious base for a relaxing break away from it all. The facilities at this modern 58-bedroom hotel are simply superb, with the emphasis placed on complete guest comfort. All the guest rooms are en-suite and beautifully furnished, with every facility you need and for a special treat you can book into one of seven executive suites which boast their own jacuzzi and king size bed. In the restaurant you can choose from the finest Cheshire produce cooked to perfection and should you be worried about the calories, you can work of any excesses in the comprehensive leisure complex.

Frodsham is an attractive town with a broad High Street lined with thatched cottages and spacious Georgian and Victorian houses. It was once an important coaching town during the 18th and 19th centuries and there are several fine coaching inns. Built in 1632, The Bear's Paw, with its three stone gables, recalls the bear-baiting that used to take place nearby. However, the town itself dates back to at least Norman times when the Earls of Chester built a castle here. The castle was later destroyed in the 17th century and only fragments remain on Overton Hill. Below the north face of the hill is the Church of St Laurence, with views spread out over the town, the Mersey Estuary and the Manchester Ship Canal. The church still has some fragments of Norman carving, but it is the exquisite north chapel with its 17th century panelling which is of particular note.

The Old Hall Hotel, Main Street, Frodsham Tel: 0928 732052
Fax: 0928 39046

The Old Hall Hotel is a lovely 16th century building situated right in the heart of Frodsham, opposite the Mersey Estuary. Within the grounds there are two commemorative stones dated 1862 which mark the level reached by flood waters at that time and in the gardens there is a large stone bath or well with a stepped access. The interior of the building is beautifully decorated and rather unusual, but of particular interest are the two areas of wattle and daub which have been left exposed. There are also lovely open fireplaces for added warmth in the winter. The bedrooms are extremely spacious and decorated to a high standard. All are en-suite and have colour television, telephone, and tea and coffee facilities. As well as eight single rooms, 11 doubles, and one family room, there is also a suite available. The restaurant serves breakfast, luncheon and dinner, with à la carte and table d'hôte always proving to be popular with residents. The bar is well stocked and has a friendly, welcoming atmosphere. Mr. and Mrs. Winfield have run the hotel for the past 18 years and like to provide their guests with first class standards and efficient staff. We thoroughly enjoyed our visit to The Old Hall Hotel and were delighted to have met with such friendly service.

Just south of the town, horse lovers will discover a real haven at **The Hill Top Equestrian Centre** which is set in beautiful Cheshire countryside at **Newton-by-Frodsham**, and has outstanding views of the surrounding area. Owned by Tony Faulkner, Joy Smith, a BHS Instructor has been running the riding centre for the past 18 months. As well as providing livery for horse owners, the Centre has 31 stables, an indoor and outdoor menarge and cross country fences. Riding lessons are available, catering for both beginners and experienced riders and people are encouraged to visit the Centre to watch lessons in progress and obtain expert advice on all aspects of horsemanship. Every care has been taken to provide excellent livery for the horses, and their well-being is the main priority at all times.

Hill Top Equestrian Centre, Newton-by-Frodsham Tel: 0928 788235

Lying approximately six miles west of Northwich and signposted from the A556, **Delamere Forest** is a rambler's delight, its 4,000 acres of woodland incorporating a wealth of lovely walks and various picnic sites for a peaceful family day out in the country.

In Norman times the word 'forest' meant a protected hunting ground for royalty or nobility. Delamere was originally used by the Earls of Chester and it became a Royal Forest in the 14th century, with James I being the last king to hunt deer here. Large areas of oak were cleared from the Forest in Tudor times for ship building and boat construction, as well as for the familiar black and white half-timbered cottages of Cheshire. Since the early 20th century, Delamere Forest has been under the control of the Forestry Commission, who undertook an intensive programme of tree planting and woodland management. Now very much a working forest, 90% of the trees are eventually destined for the saw mills.

Delamere Forest Inn, Blakemere Lane, Delamere Forest, Norley
Tel: 0928 788655

One place worth seeking out while you are here is the **Delamere Forest Inn**, a welcoming, traditional establishment which makes an ideal stopping-off point in any journey. Situated on the road between the A556 and **Norley**, the inn dates back to 1635 and careful refurbishment has ensured none of its original character has been lost, with exposed oak beams, roaring log fires and various pieces of bygone memorabilia enhancing a sense of times past. In addition to a fine selection of well-kept ale, you can choose from extensive lunchtime and evening menus, with something to suit every taste. If you are too weary to continue your travels for the day, there are six lovely guest rooms available, two of which have en-suite facilities, ensuring every visitor's needs are catered for.

Northwest of Norley, another pleasant walk, albeit rather steep, is the climb out of **Helsby** village along pretty woodland paths to the red sandstone summit of Helsby Hill, where you'll find the site of an Iron Age fort. The hill is now owned and protected by the National Trust.

The views from here across the Manchester Ship Canal and Mersey Estuary towards Liverpool are superb and you can still see the artificial defences on the south and east sides of the fort, together with the remains of the man-made defensive earthworks behind the triangulation point at the summit.

The Vale Royal is an area of some 150 square miles, incorporating some of the most beautiful Cheshire countryside. Within this vast area there is a wealth of historic sites revealing the rich heritage of this lovely rural county. The name originated when Prince Edward, eighth Earl of Chester declared it to be "The Vale Royal of England" because he felt it was so beautiful. Among the many places to visit there is the Anderton Boat Lift, an impressive structure recently restored to its former glory. The lift was conceived and designed by Edward Leader Williams who later found fame for designing the Manchester Ship Canal, and it played a major part in the industrial development of the area. Using amazing hydraulics this cast iron construction was a marvel of the era, literally "lifting" boats and transferring them from the river to the canal.

For the sporting enthusiast, The Vale Royal has a wide range of facilities, including Rudheath Leisure Centre, complete with sports hall, village room and fitness suite, Northwich Swimming Pool, Winsford Indoor Sports Complex with amenities for all kinds of sporting activities and Knights Grange Sports Complex which caters for a wide variety of sports ranging from golf to indoor bowls and crazy golf.

The abundance of countryside walks, meres, canals and rivers for the nature enthusiast, ensures that within this wonderful area there is something to appeal to everyone.

Vale Royal Borough Council, Wyvern House, The Drumber,
Winsford Tel: 0606 862862

Anderton Lift, Nr Northwich

Little Budworth, east of **Winsford**, is an attractive village with views over the Budworth Pool which gives the village its name - 'bode worth', or dwelling by the water. Close by is Little Budworth Country Park, consisting mainly of ancient heathland, with a mixture of heather, gorse, bracken and silver birch trees growing on sandy soil - much as they did thousands of years ago, though oaks and rowan trees are now appearing. This is an attractive area to sit or stroll in, with car parking and picnic areas. Close by is Oulton Park Picnic Area and motor racing enthusiasts are not far from the celebrated Oulton Park racing circuit.

The re-introduction of herbs is due to people such as Libby and Ted Riddell, who own and run a specialist herb nursery called Cheshire Herbs in Forest Road, Little Budworth. The main thrust of the company is the growing and selling of retail and wholesale herb pot plants, producing over 180 different varieties. The nursery boasts a herb garden where customers can see the plants in situ so as to be able to appreciate the individual stature of the plant they wish to buy. There is also a small yet comprehensive shop selling herb-related products. In the time since Cheshire Herbs have been operating, they have won gold medals for exhibiting at the Horticultural Society, the Cheshire Show, the Leicester Flower Show, the Stoke Garden Festival, the Lakeland Rose Show and the Shrewsbury Flower Show. A gold medal and diamond award was also presented to them at the Southport Flower Show. Libby is often requested to give talks on the subject of herbs, and both Libby and Ted run a series of courses during the summer months. The topics of the courses are quite far ranging and cover subjects such as 'Planning a Herb Garden'. This is a one-day course and relates the history of herbs, hints on planning a herb garden, the diversity of herbs and their use in borders.

Other courses are entitled 'Uses of Herbs', 'Growing Herbs', 'Herbs in the Stillroom', 'Hooked on Herbs' and 'Midsummer Night at Cheshire Herbs'. Libby and Ted have a wealth of literature on the subject and would be delighted to forward information to any of our readers. In one of their handouts, we discovered a lovely poem by Walter de la Mare which we have chosen to include in our book.

THE SUNKEN GARDEN

Speak not - whisper not;
Here bloweth thyme and bergamot;
Softly on the evening hour,
Secret herbs their spices shower.
Dark spiked rosemary and myrrh,

Lean stalked purple lavender;
Hides within bosom, too,
All her sorrows, bitter rue.

Breathe not - trespass not;
Of this green and darkling spot,
Latticed from the moon's beams,
Perchance a distant dreamer dreams;
Perchance upon its darkening air,
The unseen ghosts of children fare,
Faintly swinging, sway and sweep,
Like lovely sea - flowers of the deep;
Amid its gloomed and daisied sward,
Stands with bowed and dewy head,
That one little leaden Lad.

If you choose to visit Cheshire Herbs, be sure to allow at least a couple of hours in order to enjoy the fascinating world of herbs that Libby and Ted have created. For more information, telephone 0829 760578.

Cheshire Herbs, Forest Road, Little Budworth, Near Tarporley
Tel: 0829 760578

If you find yourselves on the main A49 at **Cotebrook**, Nr Tarporley, do make time to stop off at the **Alvanley Arms**. This charming red sandstone building is run by Doreen and Joe White and their three children Stuart, Sally and Chris, who have gained the pub a very well deserved reputation for a warm welcome and really good food.

Alvanley Arms, Forest Road, Cotebrook, Tarporley, Cheshire
Tel: 0829 760200

205

The building dates back to the mid 17th century and it is particularly attractive in Summer with a profusion of creepers and hanging baskets. Inside it is no less impressive with low ceilings and a log fire in winter. Here you will find everything from a quick sandwich to a full meal, all freshly prepared, and as the menu and daily specials would fill a page of this book, you can be sure of finding something to suit you. The beer here is very good too, and if you are not familiar with Robinson's ales we can say that they are excellent. A pub not to miss. One final point to note is that they have two lovely en-suite rooms available if you want to break your journey.

Vale Royal has given its name to the modern district of Cheshire in which it lies and it incorporates the Whitegate Way, a footpath that runs from Winsford to **Cuddington**, using the old railway line that carried salt from the Winsford Mines. There is a picnic site and car park at the old Whitegate Station.

The Plough, Beauty Bank, Whitegate Tel: 0606 889455

In the tiny hamlet of **Foxtwist Green** near **Whitegate**, surrounded by fields and tucked away down a No Through Road on top of Beauty Bank you will discover a very special 'hidden place' called **The Plough**. Dating back to 1910, this charming, unspoilt pub is run by jovial host Steve Buchan and his two daughters Tina and Jane. Locals and visitors mix easily here, in a homely atmosphere where fine ale and good homecooked food are the order of the day. Formerly a farm, The Plough was once part of the Delamere estate and the rear bar still features the original stoneflagged floor, making it popular with muddy-booted walkers who call in for a refreshing drink.

Not far from here lies the site of the Abbey of Vale Royal, founded by Edward I in 1277, who, according to the story, did so in fulfilment of a vow he made as Earl of Chester when crossing the Dee in a storm. As he came ashore the ship sank, but the future king was safe. It was a Cistercian monastery and once had the longest Cistercian Abbey Church in England, and after the Dissolution in the 16th century it became a country house. It is now a special school.

Travelling south, one place you are sure to want to visit is The Badger, a splendid inn situated close to the River Weaver in the picturesque village of **Church Minshull**. At one time a horse farm, later an alehouse and then a coaching inn, **The Badger** is a Building of Historic and Architectural Interest and was originally known as The Brookes Arms, after the Brookes family who were big landowners in the Mere and Tatton area. Their coat of arms bears two badgers, hence the inn's new name. The Badger's riverside location makes it popular with walkers and boating enthusiasts, particularly during the summer when full use is made of the lovely beer garden and children's play area. Inside, the warm, friendly atmosphere is enhanced by exposed brickwork and cosy alcoves and of course, badgers everywhere you look! An extensive and reasonably priced menu makes this a popular venue for a family meal out and the portions ensure you never leave feeling hungry. There are also special themed evenings including quiz nights and Hot Pot nights.

The Badger, Church Minshull, Cheshire Tel: 0270 522607

To the west of Church Minshull, **Wettenhall** is another attractive village and it is here, somewhat hidden that you will find **Wettenhall Nurseries**, a super establishment which specialises in fuschias. It can be found by taking the Wettenhall turning off the Winsford to Nantwich road, continuing for approximately two miles to the T-junction, turning right and the nurseries are on your left, just prior to the Boot and Slipper pub. Ray and Lesley Stewart are friendly proprietors who have developed a reputation for the large range of quality plants they grow and the personal attention they offer their many customers. In addition to over 500 different varieties of fuschia, the nursery provides a varied selection of plants, shrubs and trees at very reasonable prices. There is a small play area for children, plus a picnic spot and pets corner and in the nursery shop you can buy fresh fruit, vegetables and homemade ice cream.

Wettenhall Nurseries, Winsford Road, Wettenhall Tel: 0270 73376

The quaintly named **Boot & Slipper** is a real picture postcard hotel and restaurant lying adjacent to the Nurseries. Typical of its age, this 17th century black and white timbered establishment entices you inside, but beware - watch your head, for low beamed ceilings pervade throughout. This is the perfect combination of superb modern facilities in beautiful olde worlde surroundings. Patricia and Rex are welcoming hosts whose hard efforts have created a very special place, whether you want a relaxing drink, a first class meal or a super place to stay.

The Boot & Slipper Hotel and Restaurant, Long Lane, Wettenhall Tel: 027 073 238/284

There are five superbly equipped and beautifully decorated en-suite guest rooms and in the cosy atmosphere of the bar and restaurant, with feature brick faced fireplace, quarry tiled floors and lovely old style furniture, you can savour a fine selection of ale and an excellent gourmet menu.

North of here is the town of **Winsford** which, despite its growth in recent years with housing development, still retains several features of historic interest, including some timber framed pubs in the centre and an unusual timber framed church built for bargees travelling on the River Weaver. Winsford is actually formed from two older townships, **Over** and **Wharton** on either side of the River Weaver. Winford Bottom Flash is a popular area for angling, canoeing and pleasure boating.

On Station Road in Wharton, near Winsford, stands the **Oddfellows Arms**, a charming pub run by friendly hosts Norman and Samantha Temple. One of the first properties to be built in this area, the building housing the Oddfellows Arms has stood for well over 250 years and was for a long time a lodging house until it became a pub towards the beginning of the 19th century. The somewhat unusual exterior is matched by a magical interior full of character where a cheerful, welcoming atmosphere prevails. The pub is tastefully furnished in keeping with the period and provides a relaxing setting where locals and visitors mix easily, enjoying a pint of fine ale and friendly conversation.

Oddfellows Arms, Station Road, Wharton, Winsford
Tel: 0606 593643

Middlewich, another salt town, was also the site of two Civil War battles. It also lies on King Street, a Roman Road which is now the A530. In the church, dedicated to St. Michael, there are some old carvings and the coat of arms of the Kinderton family of nearby

Kinderton Hall. The crest shows a dragon eating a child and this somewhat gruesome emblem related to a legend of how a member of the family, Baron Kinderton, killed a local dragon as it was devouring a child - presumably too late to save the unfortunate youngster. A lane at Moston near Sandbach, where the incident is supposed to have taken place, is still called Dragon Lane.

Sandhurst Guest House, 69 Chester Road, Middlewich
Tel: 0606 834 125 / 833 753 Fax: 0606 836 676

Set back from the A54 on the edge of Middlewich town centre, **Sandhurst** is the impressive home of Angelika and Douglas Fair who enjoy sharing it with their many guests. Originally built in 1908 as a private dwelling for the manager of Brunner Mond, this splendid house stands in half an acre of gardens and makes an ideal base from which to explore the surrounding area. There are four warm and comfortably furnished guest rooms, two with en-suite facilities. Downstairs, the dining room provides a lovely mealtime setting with a delightful feature fireplace enhancing its period character. Angelika will readily cater for special diets with prior notice and it is immediately apparent that guest comfort is of paramount importance here.

By taking the **Warmingham** turning off the Middlewich to Nantwich road, you will find **Warmingham Grange**. Built over 180 years ago as a gentleman's residence this impressive mansion house is set in over 60 acres of beautiful pastureland. Friendly host Chris Wright came here seven years ago and through sheer hard work has created a first class establishment which caters for everyone, whether you want a relaxing drink, a delicious meal or a fun night out. King Arthur's tavern provides a welcoming atmosphere in which to savour a fine pint of ale, and in the luxurious surroundings of Lancelot's Restaurant you can enjoy a choice from an excellent à la carte menu. Galahads Nightclub is available for private hire during the week and

210

Saxon Crosses at Sandbach

is open to the public on Friday and Saturday nights, with live cabaret performances ensuring a fun night for all.

Warmingham Grange, Warmingham, Sandbach
Tel: 027077 276/412 Fax: 027077 413

Lying on the Trent and Mersey Canal which forms part of the Cheshire Ring, **Sandbach** is an ideal stopping-off point for the canal traveller. It is also readily accessible by road, situated barely a mile from the M6 motorway. In its Market Place you will find a link with Cheshire's pre-Conquest history - two richly carved Anglo-Saxon sandstone crosses, dating from between the 8th and 9th centuries and making a focal point in this attractive town.

One theory about the origin of the crosses is that they were set up when Peada, son of the heathen warrior King Penda, married the daughter of the King of Northumbria. The Princess agreed to the wedding only on the condition that she should become the Queen of Christian country. She must have been a persuasive lady, for Peada duly accepted her requirements and St. Chad and other holy missionaries came down from Northumbria to convert the ancient pagan kingdom of Mercia, which included what later became Cheshire, to Christianity.

The crosses were damaged by the Puritans but restored by a local historian, George Ormerod, in the last century and placed in their present position.

Just a few yards from the Market Square is **The Lower Chequer**, reputed to be the oldest building in the town and dating back as far as 1570. The attractive exterior of this charming black and white timbered building entices you inside into the cosy bar which is full of character and atmosphere. Sally and John Moore are first class hosts who bought this delightful freehouse a couple of years ago and since then have developed it into a popular stopping-off point with visitors

212

and locals alike.The Lower Chequer is CAMRA Recommended and you will find a regularly changing selection of Real Ales is complemented by an excellent menu of tasty bar meals and daily blackboard specials.

The Lower Chequer, Crown Bank, The Square, Sandbach
Tel: 0270 762569

Sandbach has some interesting half-timbered buildings, including the fine old 17th century Black Bear Inn with its thatched roof. The town's popular market, held every Thursday, brings people in from all over the area. It is held on Scot's Common, so called because it is the place where some of the followers of Bonny Prince Charlie were killed and buried after the battle of Worcester.

Rumours Wine Bar, 48 Congleton Road, Sandbach
Tel: 0270 763664

Travelling into Sandbach along the Congleton Road, just prior to the town centre you will find **Rumours**, a superb bistro and wine bar run by friendly proprietors Lynda and Bob. Situated within a Grade II listed building, Rumours is a real 'hidden' gem and one that proves popular with visitors and locals, so bookings are advisable, particularly at weekends. From the attractive exterior with its hanging baskets and window boxes, to the cosy and beautifully decorated interior, Rumours is first class establishment where you can savour dishes from around the globe. The menu changes daily and always includes eight vegetarian dishes, with English food always available in addition to foreign alternatives for the more adventurous diner.

Sandbach is also celebrated as the place where Edwin Foden established his world famous Foden Motor Company - when he died in 1964, his coffin was carried to its final resting place in the little church at nearby Elsworth on a steam lorry known as Pride of Edwin, which had been made in his factory at Sandbach in 1916.

Godfrey C Williams & Son, Corner House, The Square, Sandbach
Tel: 0270 762817

This charming town is the home of one of Cheshire's finest purveyors of good food. **Godfrey C. Williams and Son** was established in 1875 and since this time has gained an enviable reputation. To wander into the shop is an experience in itself, as it is reminiscent of stepping back in time to the wonderful ambience and atmsophere of a high class grocers. This speciality grocers cum delicatessen has been operating from Corner House, The Square, in Sandbach for the last 35 years. Originally the building was a coaching house, subsequently it became a tobacconist, and it now serves the local population as one of the finest grocers of quality and distinction in Cheshire. In recognition of this fact, the shop has been awarded the National Delicatessen of the Year for 1992 and 1993 by the Delicatessen and Fine Food Association. They were also finalists in the Good Cheese Shop of the Year Award.

Godfrey C Williams has seen four generations since its time of opening, and the present family consists of Mr Williams and his son. Throughout the four generations, their motto has been 'Quality always remembered when price is forgotten'. The present Mr Williams has a special affinity with both cheese and coffees, particularly Cheshire Farmhouse Cheese. This is evident from the displays in the shop. He also imports raw coffee, and is one of the few remaining grocers who roasts and blends coffee on the premises. As you can imagine, the smell wafting around in the shop is delightful. As well as cheeses and coffees, Mr Williams cooks all his own hams, and goods such as sides of smoked salmon, caviar, truffles and tinned pheasant can be purchased. It is a real pleasure to visit this remarkable shop, and like us, we are quite sure you will not be able to resist leaving without first purchasing something from the impressive range of continental and British foods on display.

The village of **Haslington** to the east of Crewe has some interesting old cottages and a small 19th century church. The old timber hall in the village was originally built by Admiral Sir Francis Vernon, one of Drake's admirals who helped defeat the Spanish Armada in 1588.

At the junction of Waterloo Road with the main road, there was until quite recently, a working blacksmith. The last horse was shod at the old smithy in 1974.

Clayhanger Hall Farm, Maw Lane, Haslington, Crewe
Tel: 0270 583952

Clayhanger Hall Farm stands on the site of a medieval hall on Maw Lane in Haslington and is the impressive home of Marlene and Dennis Hughes. Part of a 250 acre working dairy farm this charming farmhouse has been awarded 4 Q's by the AA, Highly Acclaimed by the RAC and Three Crowns Commended by the English Tourist Board, giving you some idea of the comfort and facilities you can expect here.

Former farm buildings have been tastefully converted to provide superb accommodation in four beautifully furnished and well-equipped en-suite guest rooms with lovely garden views at the front and rolling countryside to the rear. This is a very inviting holiday base with a warm, friendly atmosphere and guests are welcome to look around the farm, but children must be accompanied by an adult.

The Railway Age, Vernon Way, Crewe Tel: 0270 258923

For visitors to the area one of Cheshire's premier attractions, **The Railway Age** at **Crewe**, has something to interest the whole family. Mention the word trains and you immediately think of Crewe, indeed Crewe would not be on the map had it not been for trains. At one time, seven out of every ten men in Crewe worked on the railways, for trains did not only pass through this busy town, but were built here. At The Railway Age, you will find yourself stepping back in time to the bygone era of steam, with weekend rides available in an authentic brake van pulled by a steam locomotive on the centre's own running line. In the North Junction signal box, one of three original boxes, visitors can enjoy some "hands on" exhibits and there are further activities available for younger members of the family in the indoor Children's Corner. Although it seems sad in some ways that these giant steam engines are now no more than exhibition pieces, we should nevertheless be grateful that someone had the foresight to preserve this important part of history for everyone to enjoy.

Within a few minutes walk of Crewe town centre, but conveniently hidden adjacent to the West Coast main railway line and sited within the old Crewe Coal Wharf, is the aptly named **Sleepers Hotel**. Owners Brian and Joan Shannon have converted two old railway houses and adjoining stables dating back to the 1850s into a superb hotel and restaurant. Much care has been taken to retain as much as possible of the old structure of the properties while providing every

216

modern amenity. There are ten attractively furnished en-suite guest rooms and in the converted stable area, a cosy bar and restaurant full of character, with some of the original stalls complete with brass tethering rings, incorporated into decor. The choice of food here is excellent and very reasonably priced, just one of the many factors which makes Sleepers Hotel a wonderful place to stay.

Sleepers Hotel, The Wharf, Thomas Street, Crewe Tel: 0270 585555
Fax: 0270 585479

Barthomley, to the east of Crewe and close to the M6 motorway, is a beautiful little village, typical of so many in Cheshire with its black and white half-timbered cottages. It has a unique church dedicated to St. Bertoline, an 8th century Saxon prince who became a hermit on an island in the little River Sow in Staffordshire. It was here that a terrible massacre took place in 1643 during the Civil War, when a band of Royalist soldiers arrived in the village. The residents took refuge in the church tower, but the soldiers smoked them out with fire by burning the pews and rush mats. When the villagers surrendered, they were stripped and brutally murdered.

Dating back to the mid-17th century, **The White Lion Inn** at the nearby village of **Weston** really is a 'hidden' gem. Situated on the A531, this delightful black and white timbered building was formerly an old Tudor farmhouse and at one time a Smithy. The lounge bar still features original oak beams and is full of character and charm, providing a cosy setting for a relaxing drink and a tasty bar meal. Should you opt for the more formal elegance of the restaurant, you will be rewarded with an extensive menu of international cuisine for which The White Lion is justifiably renowned throughout the area. The sixteen guest rooms are all en-suite and superbly equipped, with extra personal touches such as complimentary mineral water ensuring maximum comfort. For those special occasions or just as a treat,

217

you can choose one of the two suites to add a taste of luxury to your stay. This delightful AA Two Star hotel is run by a friendly couple, Alison and Gordon Davies, who together with their professional team of staff have created a super place to stay. What's more, The White Lion even has its own bowling green!

The White Lion Inn, Main Road, Weston Tel: 0270 500303

The town of **Nantwich** is definitely the focal point of this part of Cheshire. This lovely old town was once second only in importance to Chester in the county, being used by the Romans as a supplier of salt for their garrisons at Chester and Stoke. It remained a salt producing town from Saxon times onwards, but production declined in the 18th century as other centres with better communications on the canal system such as Northwich increased in importance. However, a brine spring still supplies the town's outdoor swimming pool.

The Wilbraham Arms, Welsh Row, Nantwich Tel: 0270 626419

Situated on Welsh Row, just two minute's walk from Nantwich

town centre, you will find the **Wilbraham Arms**, a first class inn run by Mick and Jan Merrick. Listed with the AA and awarded a 3 Key grading, the Wilbraham Arms is an ideal stopping-off point, whether you are looking for a tasty meal, a refreshing pint of fine ale or a comfortable place to stay and Mick and Jan cater admirably for your every need. The menu is surprisingly reasonably priced and has a wide range of hot and cold dishes to appeal to every taste, accompanied by a carefully selected wine list. Mick and Jan also have their own ale brewed for them and this is the only place where you can savour the unique taste of Dabbers Gold. The Wilbraham Arms exudes a cheerful, welcoming atmosphere throughout, which extends into the eight well furnished guest rooms, two of which are en-suite.

When you are in the town, be sure to pop into **Magpie Crafts** at 44 Hospital Street. It is a charming little shop with the exterior attractively surrounded by hanging baskets and window boxes, all jammed full of the most colourful flowers and plants. Sue Adams is the proprietor, and she has been in business for seven years. The business has operated from the present premises for just four and a half years and is proving to be very successful. The exterior has a charming Victorian shop front, and immediately prior to Sue purchasing the building, the rooms at the front of the property were used as living accommodation. The interior of the shop is attractively decorated and has lovely low beamed ceilings which add to the atmosphere of the premises. Sue retails most types of crafts, ranging from hand painted designs on stained glass, to real flower gifts and miniatures of every type. Also on display are brass paperweights, pottery and paintings. We spent a very enjoyable half hour admiring the many items she has for sale, and of course could not leave without buying a little memento of our visit to Nantwich.

Magpie Crafts, 44 Hospital Street, Nantwich Tel: 0270 629808

Churche's Mansion, Nantwich

In 1583, the town was devastated by a disastrous fire which raged across the half-timbered and thatched buildings and lasted for 20 days, leaving only a few buildings standing. It is recorded that during the fire the bears kept behind the Crown Hotel were let loose and the townswomen were afraid to help with fighting the fire for fear of the beasts. Four bears from Nantwich are mentioned in Shakespeare's comedy 'The Merry Wives of Windsor'.

Fortunately a few fine old buildings did survive the fire, such as the moated half-timbered mansion in Hospital Street belonging to Nantwich merchant Rychard Churche, which was built in 1577. It is now open to the public as a small museum and is worth a visit after you have been to Magpie Crafts.

Another important Nantwich building to escape fire damage was the fine 14th century Parish Church, sometimes called the 'Cathedral of South Cheshire'. It dates from a great period of Nantwich's prosperity as a salt town and trading centre, and is richly decorated with an unusual octagonal tower. Of exceptional interest is the magnificent chancel and the wonderful carving in the choir. On the misericords (tip-up seats) are mermaids, foxes (some dressed as monks - an interesting social comment), pigs and the legendary Wyvern - half dragon, half bird, whose name is linked with the River Weaver, 'wyvern' being an old pronunciation of Weaver.

An amusing tale about the building of the church concerns an old woman who brought ale and food each day from a local inn to the masons working on site. Unfortunately the masons discovered that the woman was cheating them by keeping some of the money they put 'in the pot' for their refreshment. They dismissed her and sought revenge by carving her image in the church, being carried away by the Devil himself with her hand still in the pot. To this day, inhabitants of Nantwich are known as 'Dabbers'.

We were amused to find that Nantwich has a veritable menagerie of inns and public houses. **The Red Cow** in Beam Street is the oldest building in Nantwich. Once a 14th century farmhouse, it became an inn during the 16th century in order to cater for the drovers travelling south en-route to market. It is renowned for its excellent Real Ales, such as Robinson's Best Bitter and Mild, Hartley's XB Bitter and, an old favourite with the locals, Old Tom. Due to the popularity of The Red Cow, visitors have come from as far afield as Japan, U.S.A., Sweden and Germany. The interior is very cosy, with a beautiful inglenook fireplace, low oak beams, wattle and daub panels on the walls, and a large collection of brass ornaments. There are several little nooks and crannies where customers can enjoy a drink or eat a meal in semi-private, and a section of the inn is specifically designated for non-smokers.

Nick and Libby Casson are the proprietors, and they are extremely efficient at their job. Both are chefs, and having been in the catering trade for the last 20 years, they have plenty of expertise behind them, a fact acknowledged by The Red Cow's inclusion in the Good Pub Food Guide. The menu is wide and varied, with a first class selection available. Starters include Garlic Mushrooms, Prawn Cocktail, Chef's Homemade Paté and Corn on the Cob. The main courses represent excellent value for money, with dishes such as Homemade Steak and Kidney or Mushroom Pie, Steak, Fish, Chicken, Moussaka, Chilli and Gammon. We thought the vegetarian menu particularly innovative, with choices including Broccoli and Cream Cheese Pie, Mushroom and Nut Fettucini, Vegetable Curry, Chilli and Lasagne. Baked Potatoes with a variety of fillings, Beef Burgers and Open Sandwiches are also available if you require a light lunch and in addition to the menu there is a range of blackboard daily specials. Children are welcome lunchtimes and evenings, and a special menu is available to them, also of excellent value. There is also a large beer garden with swings and a tractor where children can amuse themselves.

For visitors wishing to stay overnight, there is adequate and comfortable accommodation in the adjoining cottage. Each room has tea and coffee making facilities and colour television. All in all, The Red Cow is one of the finest inns we have had the pleasure of visiting and we will definitely call in again when next in the area.

The Red Cow

The Red Cow, Beam Street, Nantwich Tel: 0270 628581

During the Civil War, Nantwich was the only town in Cheshire to support Cromwell's Parliamentary army. After several weeks of fighting, the Royalist forces were finally defeated on 25th January 1644 and the people of Nantwich celebrated by wearing sprigs of holly in their hair and hats. As a result, the day became known as 'Holly

Holy Day' and every year the Saturday closest to 25th January, the town welcomes Cromwellian pikemen, and battle scenes are re-enacted by members of the Sealed Knot. There are records of the Civil War and exhibitions in the Nantwich Museum in Pillory Street which also has material about the town and its dairy and cheese-making industry.

There are various attractive villages within easy reach of Nantwich, each with their particular appeal and worth exploring. **Wrenbury** to the south is a typical example, with an old church by the village green which has a corner tower that carries stairs to the top of it. The village green was used for bear baiting and it is recorded that on at least one occasion the vicar stopped the Sunday morning service when a travelling bear arrived and went outside with the congregation to see the bear being paraded around the green.

Wybunbury lies to the east and situated off the A51 can be reached easily by car. A village long before Norman times, its name derives from 'Wigbeorns Fort' (early Anglo Saxon) and in the Domesday Book it is listed as 'Wineberie', an administrative and religious centre for ten surrounding townships. However, this small village has the misfortune to be sinking, due to the natural seepage of water dissolving the saltbeds deep underground, causing the whole area to subside. The church, famous for its leaning tower and medieval monuments, has had to be entirely rebuilt nearby on firmer terrain.

Stapeley Water Gardens, London Road, Stapeley, Nantwich
Tel: 0270 628628

For anyone visiting the area there is an interesting day out to be had just outside Nantwich at **Stapeley Water Gardens**. Set in 65 acres of green belt, with ample parking and easy access for the disabled to the whole site, there is a truly surprising variety of things to see and do.

For the gardener the main centre offers over two acres undercover where, in addition to a wide selection of shrubs, roses, trees, heathers and border plants, every conceivable sundry item can be found, including gifts, furniture, houseplants and outdoor clothing. Stapeley are, naturally, also well known for their extensive range of water gardening supplies and aquatic plants. The Gardens also boast the most complete angling shop in the area as well as a large range of tropical, cold water and marine fish and equipment, and an extensive pet section ranging from birds and hamsters to chinchillas.

Stapeley also have a most reassuring policy on environmental issues. Glass, paper, metal, and garden waste generated on site are recycled. Only captive bred pets are sold. Environmental education packs are available to school parties. And Stapeley sponsors conservation days, with the likes of wildlife painter David Shepherd, alongside its craft fairs, antique shows and falconry displays.

The Palms Tropical Oasis is a vast, 1/3rd acre glass pavilion open all year round, housing exotic plants ranging from 30ft palm trees to giant Amazonian water lilies and displays from the National Begonia Collection and National Water Lily Collection. Here you can see rare and protected species of birds and animals breeding, stingray lagoon, even piranhas, or have a try at the nature quiz. Afterwards visitors can relax in the licensed Terrace Restaurant, with piano accompaniment at weekends, or the licensed Italian Garden Restaurant, both set amongst exotic flowering plants and pools, or alternatively rest in Palm Court next to the Koi pool, with its avenue of palms and a beautiful sequencing display fountain at its head.

And that isn't all; the Yesteryear Museum is a fascinating display and includes a Churchill tank, toys, agricultural antiques and fashions.

Inspired? Why not buy a copy of The Stapeley Book of Water Gardens, from the garden centre and learn how to have a go yourself?

The home of **Snugburys Ice Cream** is a 250 acre working farm consisting of 130 Friesian cows and 30 Jersey cows. Park Farm can be found just outside Nantwich on the A51, and is run by a charming couple called Mr and Mrs Sadler. The Sadlers have been making ice cream for five years now, and they told us that the quality of the product is most important to them and that their quest is to achieve perfection. Having sampled some of the delicious flavours available, we are convinced that they are close to reaching their aim. To ensure that the product maintains its quality, they go to the trouble of purchasing only top quality ingredients. For example, ginger is imported from Australia, honey comes all the way from Hungary, and the brandy used is Napoleon. As well as making superb ice cream, they also manufacture clotted cream, which can be purchased at the farm shop. In Devon, it is not unusual to see ice cream served in a cone with a large helping of clotted cream on the top, so we were delighted to learn that Snugbury's Ice Cream can also be purchased in the same way. If you haven't tried eating ice cream in this manner, we suggest you do - it really is delicious!

Snugburys Ice Cream Farm, Park Farm, Hurleston, Nantwich
Tel: 0270 624830

You don't have to be a horticultural enthusiast to appreciate the sheer natural beauty of **Bridgemere Garden World** which lies seven miles south of Nantwich on the A51. Starting out as a small nursery many years ago, this superb garden centre has grown to become one of the largest of its kind in Europe, covering 175 acres of land, 25 of which are open to the public. As its name suggests, this truly is a garden world, with something to fascinate every member of the family. In Water World you will find everything you need relating to fish and pond care, including a collection of amazingly large Koi Carp. Within the grounds, five acres have been transformed to create Garden Kingdom, where visitors can walk at their leisure through over twenty different types of garden. The Cottage Garden, full of larkspur, rosemary and lavender, the Winter Garden provides a surprising variety of plant life during the gloomier months, and the Gardener's Diary Television Garden provided the set of this popular TV series. Garden Kingdom changes constantly throughout the year, providing changing scenery from week to week, with a picture of colour everywhere you look. There are many different sections within the Garden World for everyone to enjoy, with an Egon Ronay Recommended coffee shop providing superb refreshments, a gift area with a full range of quality items ranging from beautiful tapestry work and pottery to childrens' toys, a bookshop and, during the festive season, an outstanding Christmas Grotto. With all this, plus friendly and knowledgeable staff who help you find what you are looking for and then give you helpful advice to ensure you make a success of growing it, Bridgemere Garden World really is a garden centre with a difference.

Bridgemere Garden World, Near Nantwich, Cheshire
Tel: 09365 381/239

The name **Acton**, an attractive village two miles or so west of Nantwich, means 'township among the oak woods' - a reference to Delamere Forest which once stretched this far. The church, with its large tower, was restored after the Civil War, but a Norman font survives from the earlier church, as well as an impressive tomb of William Mainwaring, a local nobleman, dating from 1399.

Close by Dorfold Hall is said to stand on the site of a hunting lodge and deer park used by Leofric, Earl of Mercia, and his wife, who is better known as Lady Godiva. The present Hall is a magnificent Jacobean country house, built in mature brick with a beautiful cobbled courtyard, with richly decorated plaster ceilings and panelling. One of the upstairs rooms has been described as one of the finest in England Another room, prepared for a visit by James I, has coat-of-arms in plasterwork and a secret cupboard for his personal possessions. Sadly, the visit of the King never took place and the expense was in vain. The gardens have lawns, woodlands and a fine avenue of old limes. An ancient oak tree in the grounds is reputed to have been the southern-most point of Delamere Forest.

As you travel along the main road out of Nantwich towards Chester, you would be well advised to stop off at **The Red Lion**, an impressive looking former coaching inn that has been providing weary travellers with welcome refreshment and accommodation for many years. Whether it's a cosy evening meal, a light lunchtime

226

snack, a pint of fine ale or a comfortable place to stay, The Red Lion caters for everyone's needs. This is a cosy, welcoming establishment which is enhanced by the warm personalities of cheerful hostess Yvonne Dodd and her friendly team of staff. There are five attractively furnished guest rooms and outside, adjacent to the large car park, there is a safe, well equipped play area for children to enjoy.

The Red Lion Hotel, Barony Road, Nantwich Tel: 0270 625424

Just off the A51, the road to Chester, and only a few miles out of Nantwich, is the village of **Barbridge**. Here, on the banks of the Shropshire Union Canal, is **The Barbridge Inn**. Until recently this pub was called The King's Arms, which was built when the canal first opened back in the mid-18th century, but has now been renamed. The old stables and smithy can still be seen on the opposite side of the canal which were used for the canal horses.

The Barbridge Inn, Old Chester Road, Barbridge, Nantwich
Tel: 0270 73443

Dorfold Hall, Nr Nantwich

Today, canal boats are still welcomed, and 24 hour mooring is provided right outside. The bar serves hand-pulled cask ales and guest beers are available in the Summer. There is a separate dining area too, overlooking the canal. The canalside garden is large and has a children's play area, and in the summer there are often barbeques. The towpath that runs past the pub is ideal for a gentle stroll after your meal.

Between Barbridge and Tarporley is the village of **Bunbury**. With its twisting streets and mixture of styles and periods, Bunbury might be called a typical Cheshire village. With everything from timber-frame Tudor to Georgian brick it is certainly a pleasant place to stroll around. The village grew around the church with expansion in Tudor times and when the common land of Bunbury Heath was enclosed. The village church certainly has a very interesting history. In the 14th century, Sir Hugh Calveley established a college in the church, some two hundred years later the tower was added to, together with battlements and the Ridley family chapel. Restored in Victorian times it suffered during World War II when a stray German bomb removed the roof. Luckily the church's two most important monuments escaped unscathed: one to Sir Hugh Calveley and the other to Sir George Beeston. Sir George lived over a hundred years, fighting in the army of Henry VIII in France and sixty years later commanding the warship Dreadnought in the battle against the Spanish Armada at the ripe old age of 89!

Tarporley, to the northwest of Nantwich, was an old forest town where the ancient foresters or forest wardens lived. In Utkington, just north of the village, is an old farmhouse and a Hall which has a column formed by an ancient forest tree, its roots still in the ground. The Hunting Horn of Delamere was once hung on this column as a symbol of authority for the foresters. It is now kept at the Grosvenor Museum in Chester.

Home of the Tarporley Hunt, the oldest Hunting Club in the country, **The Swan Hotel** can be found on the main street of the town. The hotel is one of only two buildings officially permitted to use the heraldic insignia originated by Queen Margaret of Anjou, consort to King Henry VI and worn as a token of loyalty by the Cheshire gentry of the Lancastrian forces at the battle near Market Drayton in 1459. The oldest part of the hotel, the Kitchen Bar, dates from 1565 and features the insignia of the Fettered White Swan. Sadly destroyed by fire in 1735, this important staging post on the London-Chester-Holyhead route was rebuilt and the Georgian facade added in 1789. Awarded a Three Crowns grading, The Swan is still a very popular stopping-off point and its historic character is enhanced by half wood panelled walls, open fireplaces and, in some of the 14 beautifully furnished, en-suite guest rooms, four poster beds. Open daily for morning coffee and afternoon teas, non-residents can also make use of the superb restaurant with its outstanding cuisine.

The Swan Hotel, 50 High Street, Tarporley Tel: 0829 733838
Fax: 0829 732932

Also on the High Street, antique lovers will discover a veritable haven when they call in at **Tarporley Antiques Centre**. This is a browser's paradise, set on two floors crammed full with pieces of antique and reproduction furniture and household items of the highest quality including pictures, prints, pottery, glassware, brass and books.

Tarporley Antiques Centre, 76 High Street, Tarporley
Tel: 0829 733919

The name 'antique centre' can be off-putting, so often associated with the wealthier classes, but Tarporley Antique Centre is one of those all too rare places where there is something to suit every taste and, more importantly, every pocket. Having been enticed in to look at the vast array of goods on display, there is sure to be something to tempt you and you will find it very hard to leave empty-handed.

The western side of Cheshire approaching the Welsh border begins to have the feel of border country, where ancient tribal feuds and wars between Saxon and Celt have their memory in the great castles of the Warlords of the Marches, which were designed to defend disputed territory. Positioned on a craggy cliff towering over the Cheshire Plain, **Beeston Castle** just south of Tarporley is a major landmark. It is reputedly the site of some buried treasure left there by King Richard II, although no gold or jewels have ever been discovered. The castle's fascinating history spans 2,500 years and the present fortress goes back to 1220, when it was built by Earl Randle, Seventh Earl of Chester, as protection against the army of the Welsh Prince, Llewellyn the Great. Now in the care of English Heritage, it is open to the public and its hilltop location provides the most spectacular views of the surrounding countryside.

Peckforton Castle, visible from Beeston, has a very different history, its purposes being far from military. It is a grand Victorian mansion, occupying a three and a half acre hilltop site. It was built between 1844 and 1851 in exact Norman style to the designs of the architect Anthony Salvin, for Lord Tollemarch, Member of Parliament for Cheshire between 1841 and 1872.

Described by the Victorian architect Sir George Gilbert Scott as 'the largest and most carefully and learnedly executed Gothic mansion of the present', Peckforton Castle with its 60 foot high towers is a fantasy in stone. It has been superbly restored and is now open to the public with guided tours, refreshments and a speciality shop.

Cholmondeley Castle, is a beautiful 19th century castle. The castle is not open to the public, but the grounds are, and visitors can enjoy superb ornamental gardens, a lakeside area, a home farm with rare breed animals and an ancient private chapel. The grounds are open on Sunday afternoons in the summer months and refreshments are available.

On the A49 at **Cholmondeley** if you follow the road opposite the Cholmondeley Arms and continue for about two and a half miles, you will discover a super place to stay at **Manor Farm**, the charming 17th century home of Jan and Tony Dilworth. This working dairy farm is set within 60 acres of beautiful countryside and Jan and Tony have totally refurbished and renovated the former cowsheds and haylofts to create both a new home for themselves and three excellent guest rooms, beautifully furnished throughout with period antiques and

Gatehouse, Beeston Castle

Cholmondley Castle

lovely fabrics enhancing a cosy, relaxed atmosphere. For visitors seeking that special country retreat, Manor Farm is ideal.

Manor Farm, Egerton, Malpas Tel: 0829 720 261

The A41 leads from Whitworth to Chester and it is worth deviating from the main road every so often in order to explore the various little villages in this attractive corner of West Cheshire.

Malpas is one of the most delightful old villages in Cheshire, though its Norman French name implies that it once lay in difficult border terrain - 'mal passage'. There was once a castle in the town, the seat of one of the Norman barons, the site of which can be seen behind the red sandstone church as a grassy green mound. There is an ancient village cross on steps, and some charming black and white cottages as well as elegant Georgian houses. In the 18th century, the village belonged to the Cholmondeleys, who built the town's almshouses.

Travelling out of Chester on the A41, if you take the first turning right after the **Broxton** roundabout, signposted for **Tilston**, then turn left at the T-junction, about half a mile on your left you will discover a rare gem called **Well House Antiques**. Formerly a pub with stables dating back to the 17th century, this magnificent building is now the home of Sally French-Greenslade and provides the perfect setting for a wonderful antique business and a museum of articles from the late 19th century. The museum includes a parlour c.1870, a bedroom and a children's playroom with a delightful feature dolls house. Sally also opens her beautiful hidden garden to the public under the National Gardens scheme, but you are advised to ring if you wish to visit the garden or museum.

Well House Antiques, Tilston, Malpas Tel: 0829 250

Dating back to the early 19th century, the **Fox and Hounds** in Tilston was formerly a farmhouse and blacksmith's before becoming an alehouse and later a pub. With outstanding views all around, this charming establishment exudes an air of peace and tranquility. Chris and Penny Hanmer are super hosts who in the short time since they moved into the Fox and Hounds have turned it into the perfect family pub, where you can savour excellent homecooking and a fine selection of ale. In the summer months you can relax outside in the picnic corner while the children run off their energy in the play area.

The Fox and Hounds, Tilston, Near Malpas, Cheshire
Tel: 0829 250255

Close to Tilston lies the small village of **Stretton** and here in glorious, peaceful countryside you'll discover Stretton Mill, a beautiful little water mill that has been carefully restored and is now open to the public. The wooden mill machinery dates back to the 18th century and is the oldest in Cheshire. Visitors can enjoy guided tours of the mill where they will be given demonstrations of how grain is ground, and in the nearby stable block, fascinating displays and models reveal the mill's history and workings. The mill is open Tuesdays to Sundays from 2pm till 6pm, from 1st March to 31st October. There is a shop and picnic area, and group visits are most welcome if booked in advance.

Lying east of the A41, the **Cheshire Candle Workshops** in **Burwardsley** is easy to find and provides a very enjoyable and interesting day out for both adults and youngsters alike. The owner of this thriving craft centre is Mr. James, and he has succeeded in creating a flourishing business of no small means. The buildings have been on the site since 1830 and are situated right in the heart of the Cheshire countryside in a setting surrounded by medieval castles. The popularity of the place will be evident by our telling you that during the last year, over 2,000 coach parties visited the premises. A visit here is a unique experience steeped in history, and proves to be exciting for all the family. If the children's attention should stray a little while Mum and Dad are watching the candles being made, there is a large play area for them to amuse themselves in.

Jacqueline is responsible for making the candles for special occasions to the client's specification. We thought this was a super idea for personal presents, birthdays, anniversaries and weddings. As well as the art of Candlemaking, there is also a Glass Studio. Rod Beckhurst runs this craft shop, and he has been making glass ornaments of every description for the past 37 years. Like Jacqueline, Rod will also happily accept private commissions for special gifts, and when you are buying a gift for someone special, it is always rather a nice touch actually to watch the article being made. Exquisitely made jewellery can also be purchased, and although we were unable to meet Beverley Edwards who makes it, we were delighted with what we saw set out on her stall.

Cheshire Workshops, Burwardsley, Near Chester Tel: 0829 70401

As well as much to see, there is also a restaurant which serves a variety of delicious meals. Called The Hayloft, it is furnished in the traditional 'olde worlde' style. Originally it served its purpose as an old Granary and Coach House. Now it is possible to enjoy a simple cup of tea or coffee, a light snack, or a full à la carte meal. It is reasonably priced and there is also a children's menu available. Of the two dining rooms, the upper floor will seat as many as 50 or 60 people and has a side room which can cater for as many as 60 or more. It is possible to book the lower dining area for coach parties with prior notice, and a further 100 seats are available here. The workshops are attractively laid out and enable visitors to browse at their leisure whilst watching the individual crafts being made. There is so much to see and do here that we know you will enjoy this hidden place with its many attractions.

Nearby, at **Gatesheath** just outside **Tattenhall**, **Country World** at New Russia Hall, a converted early Victorian farmhouse, is another place well worth stopping off at. Within this charming old building you will discover a vast range of beautiful crafts and gifts, including handmade jewellery, clothing and leather goods, plus one of the country's largest Dried Flower Workshops. Children will particularly appreciate the one acre Animal Paddock, where they can make friends with rare breed bantams, pigs, Shetland ponies and wildfowl and for the younger ones a play area is available. The Farmshop offers a wide selection of fresh produce, farmhouse cheeses, local ice cream and other edible goodies to take home after your day out and after browsing at your leisure, take time to call in at The Old Cheese Room, a café serving specialist teas and coffees, and tasty homemade meals and snacks.

Country World, New Russia Hall, Chester Road, Gatesheath,
Near Tattenhall Tel: 0829 71070

The ancient Walled City of **Chester** lies on the border with North Wales and has been welcoming visitors since Roman times. This is a city with a rich and colourful heritage and a wealth of historic buildings and great treasures from the past.

This is where mighty Roman armies built the Fortress Deva and surrounded it with the famous city walls to defend it against attacks by ferocious Welsh tribes. Today, thousands of visitors to Chester walk the two-mile circuit of the walls, taking in the splendid views of the city's illustrious past which is etched in the architecture of each building.

Your tour of the walls will take you past the largest Roman Amphitheatre ever uncovered in Britain, the site of extravagant festivals watched by 7,000 spectators and a training ground for

236

The Rows, Chester

Roman legionaries. Another beautiful sight is the city's Cathedral which celebrated 900 years of history in 1992 with various events including a production of the Chester Cycle of Mystery Plays.

For visitors to Chester looking for a comfortable holiday base, you would be well advised to seek out **Green Gables Hotel** on Edersley Park, a cosy, welcoming establishment run by friendly hostess Mrs. Purvo.

Green Gables, 11 Edersley Park, Chester Tel: 0244 372243

Within the city walls there are plentiful treasures to discover. The unique world famous two-tiered galleries of shops known as The Rows, line both sides of the main street and date from the Middle Ages. Here you will find a wide range of high class shops, restaurants and cafés, all inviting exploration.

The beautifully ornate Eastgate Clock has been watching over this scene since 1897 and apart from Big Ben in London, is probably the most photographed timepiece in the world. If your own timing is right, you might be lucky enough to witness the Town Crier giving a resounding message to everyone within earshot! If your ears can stand it, you can also join the city's resident loudspeaker for a leisurely stroll through the streets.

Enjoying a delightful location within the City Walls, where cobbled streets and lamplit alleyways create an olden day ambience, The **Chester Town House** makes a luxurious base from which to explore this beautiful, historic city.

The Chester Town House, 23 King Street, Chester Tel: 0244 350021

There is much to see and do in Chester and an ideal way to make the most of your visit is to join one of the many sightseeing tours given by a Blue Badge guide, which depart daily from the Tourist Information Centre, the Town Hall (even on Christmas Day!) and regularly from Chester Visitor Centre which can be found opposite the Amphitheatre. During summer months you can witness Caius Julius Quartus, a Roman legionary in shining armour escorting a Wall Patrol around the Fortress of Deva and recreating the life and times of a front-line defender of the great Roman empire.

After the sun has set, if your nerves can stand it, you can join in the Ghosthunter Trail, a night-time journey around the eerie haunts of Chester, exploring its mysterious and murky past and revisiting scenes of macabre events and spine-chilling happenings!

Having worked up an appetite, lovers of good food would do well to seek out **The Abbey Green Restaurant**, the 1990 Cheshire Res-

Chester Town Hall

taurant of the Year which is also Egon Ronay recommended. Here in beautifully elegant surroundings you can tempt your palate with gourmet cuisine that would satisfy the most discerning gastronome.

Abbey Green Restaurant, Rufus Court, Off Northgate Street, Chester Tel: 0244 320004

Among the many places worth visiting is The Grosvenor Musum which houses exhibitions chronicling the Roman occupation of Chester, as well as outstanding collections of paintings and silver. You can discover more about the city's fascinating past through exciting audio-visual shows at Chester Heritage Centre, while for a taste of nostalgia, the Toy Museum in Lower Bridge Street is a veritable treasure-house of antique playthings from every age, including the largest collection of Dinky and Lesney vehicles in the world.

Also on Lower Bridge Street, you will find **Clavertons**, a delightful restaurant and wine bar, popular with visitors and local alike, where you can savour a wide variety of tasty food and a refreshing drink in warm, welcoming surroundings.

Clavertons, Lower Bridge Street, Chester Tel:0244 319760

As you wander through the city streets, you will soon see why Chester is renowned for its shopping, with many shops retaining the magnificent architecture and elegance of a bygone era. However, there are more than just familiar High Street names here; Chester also has a great number of specialist and antique shops to appeal to the habitual browser looking for something a little different.

As with its shops, Chester offers a cosmopolitan choice of food, ranging from traditional half-timbered English inns, to Cantonese, French and Cajun restaurants and chic wine bars, all of which offer cuisine of the highest standard. For a real taste of Chester, look out for Cheshire Cheese and fresh Dee salmon.

For that special meal out, make your way to **Chesters Restaurant** on Lower Bridge Street, where you can savour a varied and imaginative menu that caters for the discerning customer who is looking for something a little different.

Chesters Restaurant, 58/60 Lower Bridge Street, Chester Tel: 0244 310854

Despite its long and varied history, Chester is by no means left behind in the Dark Ages, for in addition to its rich heritage and many ancient features, it also provides many modern attractions, including multi-screen cinemas, theatre and cabaret, plus concerts, ten-pin

Chester Waterfront, River Dee

bowling and a leisure centre for the sporting enthusiast.

If you are looking for a place to stay, conveniently located on City Road, **The Belgrade Hotel** makes an ideal holiday and touring base and offers very comfortable accommodation in warm, friendly surroundings.

The Belgrade Hotel, City Road, Chester Tel: 0244 312138

Another example of the cosmopolitan choice of restaurants in Chester, lovers of all-American food will find a real haven at **What's Cooking** on Grosvenor Street. Here a superb menu includes temptations such as Down on the Bayou, Dixie Chicken and Earth Wind and Fire. Well worth a visit, this is a highly popular place with visitors and locals alike.

What's Cooking, 14 Grosvenor Street, Chester Tel: 0244 346512

Of course, no visit to Chester would be complete without a trip to **Chester Zoo**. Lying outside the city and signposted off the A41 at Upton, this is Britain's largest garden zoo, set in 110 acres of landscaped grounds. Open all year round, except Christmas Day, this is definitely the place to come for a fun family day out. The mono-rail system gives visitors an exciting ride across the zoo and an alternative view of the residents and to make life even easier, you can hire wheelchairs, pushchairs and child reins should you wish.

CHAPTER NINE

Cheshire Peaks and Plains

Marton Church

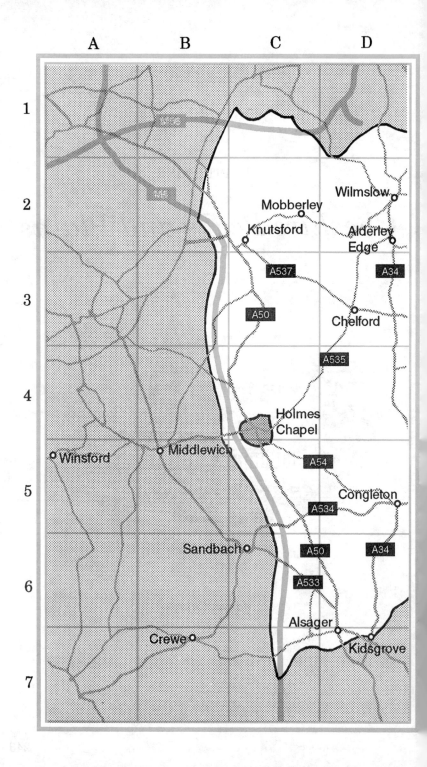

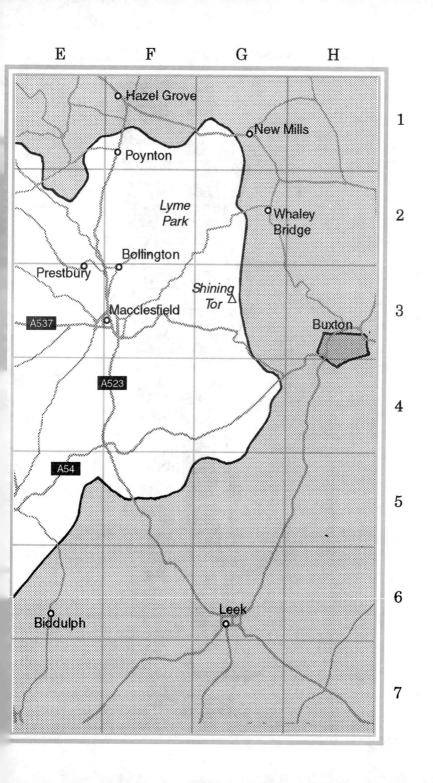

Tatton Hall

Cheshire Peaks and Plains

East Cheshire is often referred to as 'Cheshire Peaks and Plains' to indicate the contrast between the high hills to the east and the gently undulating pastures and woods on the edge of the Cheshire Plain to the west.

The contrast is sudden. Within half a mile you can find yourself travelling out of lowland Cheshire into some of the highest and wildest countryside of the Peak District - acres of lonely moorland and gritstone crags through which steep valleys and moorland streams wind their way. On the summits of the bare and empty uplands you can enjoy a sense of grandeur and wide open space almost without equal in England.

This is part of Cheshire which has a magic of its own, especially for the rambler. You can cross an expanse of open moorland to drop suddenly down quiet hillsides into intimate valleys, or climb steep ridges and summits from where you can enjoy breathtaking views back across lowland Cheshire and across to the Shropshire hills. It was here, in the deeply cut valleys on the edge of the Peak, in towns like Bollington and Macclesfield, that the early textile mills, powered by fast flowing moorland streams and serviced by the new Macclesfield Canal, heralded a new industrial world. You'll find villages of weavers' cottages and industrial terraces close to the mills they served.

South of Macclesfield is **Congleton**, an historic town, still known locally as the Bear Town.

It is thought to have its origins in Neolithic times and Stone Age people probably built the chambered tomb known as the Bridestones, the remains of which can be seen on the hill road to Leek.

There is a story that when the town bear died, the Elizabethan townsfolk lent 16 shillings to the Bear Warden for the purchase of a new one. The money had originally been collected to buy a town bible, hence the ditty: "Congleton rare, Congleton rare, sold the bible to buy a bear." Congleton was in fact one of the last towns in England to end the cruel practice of bear baiting.

Bear baiting apart, Congleton has a fascinating history. It was once an important medieval market town. It is also one of the few towns in Cheshire to keep its original medieval street pattern. The two oldest buildings are the White Lion Inn on the High Street and the Lion and the Swan Inn on West Street, both dating from the 17th century. The former was believed to have been used as an office by John Bradshaw, the High Steward of Congleton and later President of the Court that tried Charles I. There is also an impressive Venetian Gothic Style Town Hall built in 1866, which contains some interesting exhibits including a bridle for nagging wives that could be fastened to a wall in the market place! Pay a visit, too, to Congleton Park, venue for the famous Congleton Carnival and renowned for its floral plaques.

Congleton developed as an important textile town in the 18th century with many of the mills involved in silk manufacture, cotton spinning and ribbon weaving. You can still see part of Congleton's oldest silk mill at Mill Green near the River Dane.

Just south of Congleton is the village of **Astbury**. Its redbrick and black and white cottages grouped round the village green are quite a contrast from the grey-brown villages of the Peak. In Spring the green sports a thick carpet of daffodils. The splendid recessed spire of St. Mary's Church, that dominates the village, is considered one of the most striking in Cheshire. As you approach the church, you see that the spire is in actual fact detached from the nave. Though the church dates from pre-Norman times, the present building was erected between the 13th and 15th centuries and the spire was only added towards the end of construction. Beautiful timber work inside the building has made the church justifiably famous. A richly carved ceiling complements the intricate tracery on the rood screen and the lovely Jacobean font cover.

Astbury Meadow Garden Centre, Newcastle Road, Astbury
Tel: 0260 276466

While in this picturesque village it is well worth calling in at

Town Hall, Congleton

Mow Cop Castle

Astbury Meadow Garden Centre, one of four "Garden Centres of Cheshire", which can be found on Newcastle Road. Situated in the heart of beautiful Cheshire countryside, great care has been taken in the design and layout of the Centre which is set around the original shippons of a dairy farm and offers visitors a wealth of indoor and outdoor plants to choose from throughout the year. There is a wide choice of competitively priced garden and patio furniture, plus gardening equipment and tools, and for the browser there is a comprehensive gift and bookshop. On fine days you can relax beside one of the natural ponds and if you feel like some refreshment, the coffee shop serves a large selection of tasty homemade snacks.

Little Moreton Hall lies approximately three miles south of Astbury, just off the A34 and is undoubtedly one of the finest black and white timbered and moated Manor Houses in England. Ralph Moreton began its construction in about 1480 and the fabric of this magnificent house has changed little since the 16th century. Huge carved overhanging gables and distorted panels create a kaleidoscope of black and white patterns. A richly panelled Great Hall, parlour and chapel show off superb Elizabethan plaster and wood work. There is also a beautifully reconstructed Elizabethan knot garden with clipped box hedges and a period herb garden.

It is only a short drive from here to the Staffordshire border and the National Trust property of **Mow Cop**, a mock castle ruin. The location, on a hill 1100 feet above sea level, marks the beginning of the Staffordshire Way footpath. On a clear day the views are fantastic, you can see to Alderley Edge and beyond to Manchester to the north, north-east to the Peak District, south to Cannock Chase and Shropshire and west to Wales and the Berwyn Mountains.

For a day trip with a difference, pay a visit to the Steamer Pier at Damhead which lies to the east and just over the border in Staffordshire. Take a step back in time as you board **The Steamboat Swan**, a fifty year old boat driven by a 100 year old steam engine. The boat makes regular daily tours of **Rudyard Lake**, a picturesque lake which was artificially created in 1797 to feed both the Caldon and the Trent & Mersey canals. Known as the Windermere of the Midlands, it is thought that the parents of Rudyard Kipling met on a picnic outing here and that is why they later gave their son his unusual Christian name. As you tour the lake at a leisurely pace, refreshments are provided on board and you can also book special morning or evening trips, with a catering service available for the evening trips.

Rudyard Lake Steamboats, Bridge House, Windmill Street,
Macclesfield tel: 0625 612743

The A54 from congleton to **Holmes Chapel** follows the natural route of the Dane Valley. Holmes Chapel itself is a small town. It has an interested village street and a church that dates from the 15th century.

About three miles from Holmes Chapel you will find the award-winning **Jodrell Bank Science Centre** and Tree Park, whose two vast radio telescopes dominate the skyline creating a major Cheshire landmark. The Lovell Radio Telescope is the second largest, fully steerable telescope of its kind in the world. The same size as the dome of St. Paul's, it receives radio waves from space 24 hours a day.

Being both exciting and educational, a trip to Jodrell Bank provides hours of fascinating fun for the whole family. You can take a tour of the Universe with Sir Isaac Newton, or enjoy an in-depth look at the Solar System in the darkened Planetarium, discover what electro-magnetic waves can do, or send the Earth around the Sun in the Gravity Hollow. Outside in the 35 acre Arboretum you can follow the various trails and see numerous wonders of nature, before perhaps stopping to enjoy a picnic within these attractive wooded surroundings.

Lying adjacent to Jodrell Bank, **Bridge Farm** makes an excellent touring base from which to explore the rural beauty of Cheshire and its many attractions. This charming 300 year old farmhouse is part of an 120 acre arable farm owned and run by Chris and Anne Massey, a friendly couple who enjoy welcoming guests into their home all year round. There is a large garden and families are most welcome. There are three spacious and comfortable guest rooms and Anne's substantial farmhouse breakfast provides the perfect start to a day's exploring. Below the house are 12 acres of beautiful pastures farmed in a traditional manner, under the direction of the National Stewardship Scheme. There are over 100 species of wild flowers and grasses and an abundance of wildlife and visitors are very welcome to take walks in this lovely area and other parts of the farm depending on the crops.

Bridge Farm, Blackden, Holmes Chapel Tel: 0477 71202

Travelling northwards the A50 to Knutsford is a delightful road, taking you through some beautiful countryside. Just off to the east is **Peover Hall**, a Tudor manor house dating from 1585. The stables have some remarkable plaster-work ceilings and are worth a visit. The gardens, which are contemporary with the Hall, are enclosed by a topiary hedge.

The village of **Lower Peover** is really two separate villages a half a mile apart. Pronounced 'Peever' the village consists of a clutch of thatched, half-timbered cottages around a green, and another group

252

along a cobbled lane to the south. The second group includes the church, inn and two school buildings, and a sign on the green proclaims it to be the centre of the village. The original School is now a private house and carries a plaque in latin proclaiming it was built for humble scholars and dedicated to God and the church in 1780, it also retains the bell on the roof which would ring to call the children to their lessons.

The Church of St. Oswald dates back to 1269 and was built using a massive timber frame with complex cross-bracing, the stone tower was added some three hundred years later. It is one of the few remaining timber-framed churches in England. The interior has a some wonderful examples of carved wood and a rather unusual medieval chest, hewn from a single oak trunk. Local legend has it that girls who wished to marry local farmers would have to lift the heavy lid with one hand to show they were strong enough to make worthy farmers wives. Across from the church is the village pub, **Bell's of Peover Inn**, The name has little to do with the church bells but rather refers to a former landlord called Bell.

The village itself can be reached off the B5081 and a short walk along either The Cobbles or Church Walk.

Cottage Restaurant and Lodge, London Road, Allostock, Knutsford
Tel: 0565 722470

A popular stopping-off point, nestling in the midst of the rolling Cheshire countryside between Knutsford and Holmes Chapel, is **The Cottage Restaurant and Lodge**. Although its situation is on the main A50, nothing could be further from crowds and traffic for an enjoyable and secluded visit to this area. As the name suggests, The Cottage was originally an old Cheshire cottage that has been taste-fully renovated and extended to give a delightful blend of the old and the new. The Cottage is under the personal management of the

253

owners, Alan Hopkin and Fred Fletcher who will be pleased to welcome guests, either for a simple bar snack lunch, a gourmet dinner or even longer stay. All food is prepared on the premises by well renowned chefs, using only the best fresh ingredients. The ambience of the candle-lit dining room does full justice to the dinner, as does the conservatory to the summer luncheon. An excellent wine list is available, catering for all tastes and pockets. For the traveller, the twelve rooms are all extremely well-fitted and appointed, with certain accommodation being specially adapted for ease of use by those who need to use wheelchairs.

The attractive market town of **Knutsford** lies on the edge of gentle lowland countryside off the A556. Dating from medieval times it retains a certain quaintness and olde worlde charm, its narrow streets lined with a variety of fine shops, pubs, restaurants, and splendid Georgian houses.

One of the best known of the restaurants is **La Belle Epoque** which offers outstanding French cuisine. The charming building in which it is housed has an Art Nouveau interior and is the work of Richard Harding Watt who admired the Mediterranean architecture which he saw in his travels. The building was originally named the King's Coffee House, and was an idealistic social endeavour to ween the working man away from the pub by providing concerts, debates and even 'a warm bath at any hour' for sixpence. A walk along Moorside will reveal more Watt architecture together with recent interpretations of Watt's style.

During the 18th century Knutsford rapidly developed into a major coaching town on the main London-Liverpool route and not surprisingly still has many former coaching inns. However, it is as the setting for Elizabeth Gaskell's novel 'Cranford' that the town is probably best known. The novel is a chronicle of the daily events and lives of the people of a small Victorian country town, written with a blend of sympathy, sharp observation and gentle humour which still delight readers today.

If you are using Knutsford as a base, we suggest using the **Longview Hotel**, on Manchester Road overlooking the heath as an excellent place to stay. Choose from their menu of everchanging award-winning dishes. Make your reservation of 0565 632119.

An interesting feature in the town is **The Heritage Centre** in Tatton Street which opened in 1989. This is a reconstruction of a 17th century timber framed building which had been a Smithy in the 19th century. During the restoration, the old forge and bellows were found in a remarkable state of preservation. It was The Macclesfield and Vale Royal Groundwork Trust who undertook the rebuilding, using

Jodrell Bank, Nr Holmes Chapel

original materials wherever possible. The wrought iron gate which leads up into the courtyard in front of the Centre was designed as part of an environmental art project and depicts dancing girls taking part in the local May Day celebrations - another popular tradition that continues today.

The festivities of Royal May Day, which are considered the most impressive of their kind in England, began in 1864 and earned their Royal prefix when the town was visited by the Prince of Wales in 1887. The celebrations consist of Maypole dancing and a large procession headed by Jack in Green and the May Queen in a horse-drawn landeau. All vehicles are banned from the town centre and the streets are carpeted with coloured sand in which patterns are traced.

While you are shopping, or just exploring the pretty streets, you could stop for a cup of coffee or a bite to eat at **The Courtyard Coffee House** at the rear of 92 King Street. They are open seven days a week, from 10 to 4.30. Their claim to fame is that they are the first Pennyfarthing museum.

Just outside Knutsford on the A5033 stands **Tabley House**. The Tabley Estate was the home of the Leicester family from 1272 to 1975 and today is open to the public who come in their droves to see the many treasures it houses. There is an outstanding collection of paintings by numerous well known artists, including JMW Turner, Henry Thompson, Dobson, Lely, Reynold, Cotes and many others besides. These have been rehung in the restored rooms of the main floor and, together with a beautiful collection of Chippendale, Bullock and Gillow of Lancaster furniture, provide an awesome sight.

A visit to the renowned **Tatton Park** which lies just outside the centre of Knutsford heading towards Rostherne, has always been regarded as one of the best days out in the North West and is not surprisingly the National Trust's most visited property. It is the complete historic country estate. A magnificent Georgian Mansion by Wyatt rises from the glorious gardens, widely regarded amongst England's 'Top Ten'. The opulent staterooms contrast with the stark servants' rooms and cellars, working as they did for the Victorian household of the noble Egerton family.

Tatton has a history stretching back to 8000 B.C., when man hunted deer for food and clothing. Eight hundred red and fallow deer still roam the 1,000 acres of parkland and round the two lakes. Tatton's history and variety of historic buildings provide the means to interpret the visitors' day out out as 'A Story for Every Age' which, as you go from one attraction to another, explains by means of boards, leaflets and guides, the relationship of the farm to the mansion, the development of the landscape and so forth. Tatton can be regarded, historically speaking, as a typical country estate, but the evidence of early occupation by man precedes 18th century emparkment which makes Tatton all the more fascinating and exceptional.

The original breeds of animals still live down on the **Home Farm**, a short walk from the Mansion - working as it did in the 1930's, the farm is the heart of the estate, with its workshops and old estate office. A 'new' steam engine has recently been restored in the engine house.

Old Hall nestles in a wood in the deer park. Visitors are given a guided tour through time from the late Middle Ages up to the 1950's. Flickering light from candles reveals the ancient timber roof of the Great Hall, supported by ornate quatrefoils. Underfoot, the floor is strewn with rushes, providing a warm place for the medieval Lord of the Manor and his servants to sleep. Built around 1520, Old Hall conjures up a hauntingly real image of an authentic journey through history.

To complete the day's enjoyment, visitors can take lunch in the restaurant. Many public events are held indoors and outside in the Park, ranging from a giant classic car show to classical concerts. Also of interest is the Japanese Koi Carp Show and many craft fairs. The children's adventure playground is specially tailored for pre-school up to twelve year olds and children can happily amuse themselves while parents relax in the picnic area. If you would like to telephone Tatton Park for further information prior to your visit, the 24-hour information line number is 0565 750250.

Tatton Park, Knutsford, Cheshire Tel: 0565 654822

Also situated within the grounds of Tatton Park, you will find **Tattondale Stables and Carriages**. Kevin and Sonia run this unique business where horse drawn carriages are restored. Also provided on the site are horse drawn carriage rides around the park itself. A regular feature is to see the carriages being prepared for a local

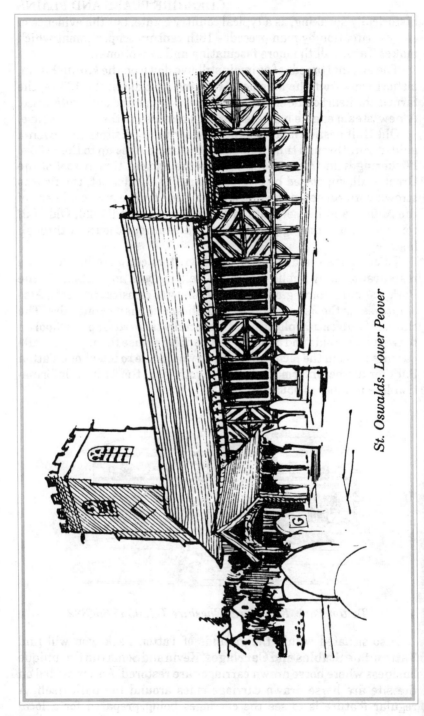

St. Oswalds. Lower Peover

wedding, just one of the few special occasions for which they are called upon to provide transport. The carriages are always turned out superbly and inevitably lend an atmosphere of elegance to any special occasion. It is not unusual to see as many as 20 horses on view in the stables, and these range from Shire horses to Shetland ponies. The Stables also specialise in beautiful Black Fresian horses which are very rare. These are indeed a sight to behold when harnessed to the carriages. Viewing is in accordance with Tatton Park's opening times during which times you can sometimes see Kevin demonstrating his skills as a wheelwright, blacksmith and farrier. He specialises in restoring and making wheels and shrinking the iron tyres onto wooden wheels. Horse riding is also available at the stables.

Tattondale Stables and Carriages, No. 2 Dairy Cottages, Tatton Park, Knutsford Tel: 0565 650618 Fax: 0565 652756

In the lovely estate village of **Rostherne** the cottages that lead up to the church are all named after shrubs and trees - apple, pear, willow, lilac and so on. At one end of the village a group of 12 house form a square. Built by estate workers in 1909, the cottages bear the crest and initials of Lady Margaret Egerton of Tatton. Lady Margaret was one of few enlightened landowners of the time and provided a bath house and laundry with irons and free soap. Up at the church the lych-gate at the western side of the church yard has an ingenious closing mechanism which uses a heavy wooden weight and pulleys. In the steeply sloping churchyard is a huge gothic-style edifice, a memorial to one Joseph Simpson, probably a rich Manchester merchant who moved out of the rapidly expanding city during the last century. To the north of the church is Rostherne Mere. At 100 acres in area and 100 feet deep it is the largest and deepest in Cheshire. According to local legend when the church bells were being hung the largest rolled across the churchyard and into the mere, and on Easter mornings a mermaid raises and tolls the bell.

To the east of Knutsford is **Wilmslow**, a busy but attractive commuter town situated on the River Bollin. It was just outside the town in an area of peat bog known as Lindow Moss that the perfectly preserved body of an Iron Age man - the famous 'Lindow Man' - was recovered. Close to the end of the high street, why not stop for a drink and a bite to eat at **The Swan**. They are a Boddingtons pub and frequently have guest beers. They also do great 'doorstep' sandwiches, fabulous burgers and their chips are the best in Cheshire.

Romany's Caravan, South Drive, Wilmslow Tel: 0625 504507

Just off the A34 in the centre of Wilmslow, adjoining the car park between Hooper's and Sainsbury's, is a small memorial garden containing **Romany's Caravan**. "Romany" was a nationally-known journalist, author and broadcaster on BBC Radio's Children's Hour in the 1930s and 40s. An ordained Methodist minister, the Reverend George Bramwell Evens retired from his ministry to Wilmslow in 1939, but continued to broadcast every week during the early war years. "Out with Romany" became the number one favourite in Request Week and his adventures in the country with his caravan ("vardo" in Romany language), dog "Raq", horse "Comma" (- never came to a full stop!) and two companions, Muriel and Doris, sustained the morale not only of children, but adults, too. Very much ahead of his time, his interest in nature has had an enormous impact on people of all kinds.

Millions mourned after his early death, in 1943, and over the years his caravan has been a place of pilgrimage not only for those who heard him, and read his books, but later generations who have discovered him either from grandparents or by reading.

Recently restored by Macclesfield Borough Council, and surrounded by Romany's favourite flowers and trees, the caravan has

King's Tower, Knutsford

once again become a favourite destination. Many of Romany's personal possessions are on display when the caravan is opened for viewing on the second Saturday in each month from May to September, from 12 - 3pm.

If you are looking for a readily accessible and centrally situated touring base from which to explore the delights of rural Cheshire, **Heatherlea Guest House** on **Lacey Green** is ideal. Friendly host Brian Smidmore provides very comfortable accommodation in five attractively furnished guest rooms, four of which are en-suite and all with tea and coffee making facilities. Located just ten minutes drive from Manchester Airport, Brian offers his guests a complimentary courtesy car service, although for those with their own transport, there is ample parking space. In addition to a full English breakfast, Brian will provide and evening meal by arrangement, or if you prefer to eat out, the centre of Wilmslow, with its wide selection of pubs and restaurants, is only ten minutes walk away.

Heatherlea Guest House, 106 Lacey Green, Wilmslow
Tel: 0625 522872

From the centre of the town you can enjoy a scenic walk through the Carrs, a pleasant riverside park, and follow the Bollin's meandering route the two miles or so to **Styal Country Park**. Owned by The National Trust, this comprises over 250 acres of woodland and riverside walks surrounding **Quarry Bank Mill**, built in 1784 and one of the first generation of cotton mills which powered by a huge iron waterwheel fed by the River Bollin. Also within the park is the delightful Styal village, which was established by the mill's original owner, Samuel Greg, a philanthropist and pioneer of the factory system. He took children from the slums of Manchester to work in his mill and in return for their labour, provided them with food, clothing, housing, education and worship.

Visitors follow the history of the mill through various galleries and displays within the museum, including weaving and spinning demonstrations, and can experience for themselves what life was like for the hundred girls and boys who once lived in the Apprentice House, with guides dressed in period costume.

It is not far from Styal to the village of **Handforth** and here on the A34 Manchester Road out of Wilmslow, you can't fail to notice **Wilmslow Garden Centre** on your left. This beautifully landscaped centre is the largest of four which make up the group known as "Garden Centres of Cheshire" and offers visitors the widest selection of plants, shrubs and garden accessories in the most relaxed surroundings. Christmas is a season which brings its own particular attractions, with a 35 feet tall inflatable Father Christmas proving popular with younger members of the family. However another equally popular and superb feature of the Centre is the extensive pet and aquatic section which specialises in fish and pets with all the associated equipment and foodstuffs. There is even a special cage which houses several chipmunks. The shop has an enormous range of cane, patio and garden furniture, barbeques and there is also a large machinery department. A superb coffee shop/restaurant provides hot and cold food, with a homemade flavour, to round off a visit.

Wilmslow Garden Centre, Manchester Road, Wilmslow
Tel: 0625 525700

The small town of **Alderley Edge** to the south of Wilmslow takes its name from a long wooded escarpment, nearly two miles in length and rising 600 feet above sea level, culminating in sandy crags overlooking the Cheshire Plain.

Alderley Edge itself is a popular area of countryside, rich in history and legend. Walkers will enjoy the network of footpaths through the woods which offer superb views of the surrounding scenery. A short walk takes you to the Wizard's Well, where you will find the following verse: "Drink of this and take thy fill, for the water falls at the Wizard's will." Local legend tells of a farmer who was on his way to Macclesfield market to sell his white horse, when he was stopped by a wizard who wished to buy the horse. The farmer refused, but he failed to sell the horse at market, and on his return was forced to sell it to the wizard. The wizard showed the farmer a cave barred by iron gates, in which a sleeping army of knights and their steeds lay ready to ride out to save the country in its hour of need. The wizard, who in some versions of the story is portrayed as Merlin, explained to the farmer that he was a horse short and he rewarded the farmer handsomely. Readers of the highly popular novels by local author Alan Garner, will recognise that

Chorley Hall, Alderley Edge

this story and the setting of Alderley Edge forms the core of his classic children's story 'The Weirdstone of Brisingamen'.

More factually, Alderley Edge once contained a large neolithic settlement and many Bronze Age tools and implements have been found here. The area is also riddled with old copper mines, some of which are dangerous and should not be explored unguided. It is now a National Trust property and a car park on the main Macclesfield road gives access to the woodlands.

From Alderley Edge a two mile walk along a footpath will take you to **Hare Hill Gardens**, a little known National Trust property situated close to the pictureque village of Prestbury. The Victorian gardens include fine woodland, rhododendrons, azaleas, a pergola and a walled garden themed in blue, white and yellow flowers. There is access via gravel paths for the less able.

Hare Hill Gardens, Alderley Edge, Cheshire Tel: 0743 709343

In **Nether Alderley**, which lies further along the A34, you'll find a delightful 15th-century watermill that has been restored by the National Trust. The red sandstone walls are almost hidden under the huge sweep of its stone tiled roof. Inside is the original Elizabethan woodwork and Victorian mill machinery which is still in working order, with two overshot wheels powering the mill. A nearby spring produces mineral water which is bottled and sold locally. If you've time, visit the 14th century church of St Mary with its unusual richly carved pew set up on a wall like an opera box and reached by a flight of steps outside.

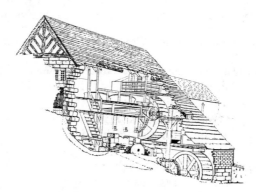

Nether Alderley Mill, Nether Alderley, Cheshire Tel: 0625 523012

Situated between Wilmslow and Macclesfield, the picturesque village of **Prestbury** is not surprisingly a regular winner of the Best

265

Kept Village title, its attractive tree-lined High Street, flanked by old coaching inns and black and white buildings which mingle with the mellow red brick work of later Georgian houses. The Church of St Peter, which dates from the 13th century, still maintains a tradition which began in 1577. A curfew bell is rung every day at 8pm during the autumn and winter, with the number of strokes corresponding to the date of the month. In the churchyard is a glass case containing pieces of carved sandstone thought to have been part of a cross erected here in the 8th century by early Saxon converts to Christianity. The fragments were discovered embedded in a wall during restoration work, where they had been hidden for 400 years. Close by is a building known as the Norman Chapel, though only the impressive doorway actually dates from Norman times. Opposite the church is a striking magpie timber-framed building which was once the vicarage. It is said that during the Commonwealth, the rightful incumbent was debarred from preaching in the church by the Puritans, and so the Rector retaliated by addressing his parishoners from the tiny balcony.

One of the charming black and white buildings on the High Street is **Ye Olde Chocolate Box**, a splendid shop bursting with wonderful gifts and mouthwatering delicacies. From its delightful black and white timbered exterior to the beautifully laid out products within and the cosy tea shop offering an enticing selection of superior snacks and beverages, this is a place oozing with olde worlde charm. A browser's paradise, Ye Olde Chocolate Box will have you lingering for hours, in a dilemma as to what to choose, but should you feel swamped by the vast array of quality soft toys, exquisite china, bulging hampers and delicious handmade chocolates, you can always take the safe option and buy your friends and relatives an exclusive gift voucher.

Ye Olde Chocolate Box, Prestbury Tel: 0625 829645

The **Bull's Head** at **Mottram St. Andrew** is located on the main through road running from Prestbury to Wilmslow. The village itself is quiet and rural and has a history dating as far back as the Domesday Book. Originally the site was a working farm with an inn attached and was converted to an inn and pub in the 1930's. Recently tastefully refurbished, the Bull's Head retains its rustic charm with genuine stone walls, beams and brasses and the atmosphere is very warm and friendly. The restaurant area has been divided into cosy alcoves on different levels and has a great reputation for its food.

The Bull's Head, Wilmslow Road, Mottram St. Andrew
Tel: 0625 828694

12' 0"
HEADROOM

Macclesfield Canal Aqueduct, Nr Congleton

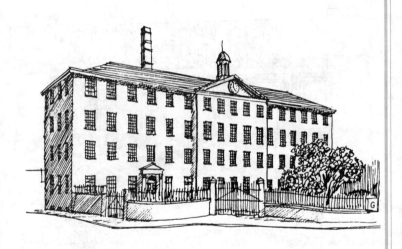

Silk Mill, Macclesfield

Macclesfield, nestling below the adjacent Peak District hills, was once an important silk manufacturing town and a market town with its origins in medieval times. The town's link with silk developed in the 17th century from a cottage industry, expanding in 1743 when Charles Roe built the first silk mill. There then followed a rapid expansion, the industry reaching its peak of activity in the 19th century. Man-made fabrics are still manufactured in the town, but textiles no longer dominate its economy.

Appropriately enough, Macclesfield has the country's only **Silk Museum**, which covers all the aspects of the silk industry, from cocoon to loom. The museum has an award-winning audio-visual presentation of the history of the Macclesfield Silk Industry and there are also fascinating exhibitions on the silk route, silk cultivation, fashion, and other uses of silk. Nearby **Paradise Mill**, which was built in the 1820s, is now a working museum demonstrating silk weaving on 26 jacquard hand looms. Exhibitions and restored workshops and living rooms capture the working conditions and lives of mill workers in the 1930s. It is also possible to buy locally made silk products at the museum.

Modern Macclesfield is an interesting town well worth exploring, with small narrow cobbled streets and alleyways, many lined with black and white timbered houses and old weavers' cottages. There is a fine market square with a market cross and, set on a hill, a handsome church that was originally founded by King Edward and Queen Eleanor. It is probably best viewed from the railway station first, before climbing the 108 steps to view its interior.

St. Michael and All Angels Church was extended at the end of the 19th century, but it retains its 14th century core. Inside is the Legh Chapel, built in 1422 to receive the body of Piers Legh who fought at Agincourt and died at the Siege of Meaux. There is also a tablet to John Brownswood, who was a schoolmaster at Stratford-Upon-Avon, and who is said to have taught Shakespeare before becoming headmaster at the local grammar school. In the Savage Chapel you'll find the famous Legh Pardon Brass, recording the medieval practice of selling forgiveness for sins.

Macclesfield Sunday School was built in 1813 for the education of local working children. It was finally closed in 1970 and as well as housing the Silk Museum, it forms the **Heritage Centre** with exhibitions on Macclesfield's rich and exciting past and on the sotry of the Sunday School itself. On the outskirts of the town is West Park Museum, a purpose-built museum founded in 1898 by the Brocklehurst family. The collection includes Egyptian artifacts, fine and decorative arts, and paintings by Charles Burnicliffe, the well known bird artist. The museum itself is set in one of the oldest public parks in England and has reputedly the largest bowling green in the country.

To the east of the town centre lies the **Macclesfield Canal**, one of the highest inland waterways in England, running for much of its length at over 500 feet above sea level. It was surveyed by Thomas Telford and opened in 1831, linking the Peak Forest Canal at Marple with the Trent and Mersey Canal near Kidsgrove, a distance of 26 miles. Between Macclesfield and Congleton, the canal descends over a hundred feet in a spectacular series of 12 locks at Bosley, before crossing the river Dane via Telford's handsome iron aqueduct. Another unusual feature of the canal is its roving bridges which carried the towpath across the canal, thus allowing horses to pass beneath the bridge before crossing it, and therefore making it unnecessary to unhitch the tow line.

At **Bollington**, the canal crosses the River Deane on a stone aqueduct, passing several of the large textile mills which it once served. Bollington grew rapidly in the 18th and 19th centuries, and in its heyday had 13 cotton mills. The Victorian shops and cottages around Water Street and the High Street give the town a marked 19th century flavour.

For the nature lover **The Middlewood Way** is a ten-mile, traffic-free country trail which follows a scenic route from Macclesfield to Marple, passing through Bollington. Open to cyclists, walkers and horse riders, this proves highly popular in the summer months and seasonal cycle hire is available, complete with child seats if required.

On the eastern side of Bollington in Church Street you will discover a lovely place to stay at **The Church House Inn**, a charming traditional 18th century inn run by Steve and Julie Robinson. The cosy bar provides a comfortable setting in which to sample a pint of fine ale and enjoy a tasty homecooked meal and on fine summer days you can take your refreshment outside in the attractive beer garden to the rear. Awarded a Three Crowns rating by the English Tourist Board and Egon Ronay recommended, The Church House provides very comfortable accommodation in five attractively furnished en-suite guest rooms and the large function room proves highly popular for wedding receptions and private parties.

The Church House Inn, Church Street, Bollington tel: 0625 574014

An interesting feature above Bollington on Kerridge Hill is White Nancy, a distincitve bell-shaped structure, erected as a monument and landmark to commemorate the battle of Waterloo in 1815. It's worth climbing up to the top (footpaths lead from the centre of town to the summit) for a magnificent view of the town with its grey mills and the great railway viaduct that cuts across the town and across the Cheshire Plain. You can continue along the ridge that forms Kerridge Hill, itself another spectacular viewpoint.

Adlington Hall, Adlington, Macclesfield Tel: 0625 829206/820201

Lovers of historic country houses would be well advised to pay a visit to **Adlington Hall**, which lies off the A523 Stockport - Macclesfield road. It has been the home of the Leghs of Adlington since 1315 and is now one of Cheshire's most popular attractions. Quadrangular in shape, this magnificent Manor House has two distinctive styles of architecture, with two sides of the courtyard and the East Wing built in the familiar black and white half-timbered fashion so common in Cheshire, whilst the later additions of the south front and west wing being of red brick.There is much to see as you tour the hall, with beautifully polished wooden floors and lovely antique furnishings enhancing the air of elegance and grandeur and each room has information packs and quiz sheets to challenge the younger visitor. The Great Hall is a magnificent sight, a vast room of lofty proportions that set off perfectly the exquisitely painted walls and the major feature, a beautifully preserved 17th century organ which was played by no less a fiure than George Frederick Handel when he visited the Hall in the mid-18th century. Outside within the lovely landscaped grounds there are various follies which are being carefully restored.

The Miners Arms, Wood Lane North, Adlington, near Poynton Tel: 0625 872731

Also in the village of **Adlington** is **The Miners Arms**. Originally this was a farmhouse and dates back to the mid-19th century. The darts area is now where the shippen once was. The building has been extended but is still made up of a series of little rooms and always feels intimate. The beer here is excellent and the food is well presented. The regular menu is supplemented by specials that are changed regularly. The conservatory-style restaurant area is non-smoking and opens onto the garden. Children will find a play area outside, and the garden is used for barbeques in the summer. The tranquil location makes this an ideal place to stop when visiting the area.

From around the 12th century, the Legh family of Adlington also had blood ties with the Legh family of nearby Lyme Park, the younger son of Thomas Legh becoming the first Piers Legh of Lyme. However, there was little or no interbreeding and the connection through later centuries was one of friendly neighbours rather than relatives, a relationship that continued even after Lyme Park had been sold to the National Trust.

Lyme Park lies half a mile west of **Disley** village on the main A6 Stockport to Buxton road and provides a fun and fascinating day out for the whole family. Set within 1377 acres of deer park, moorland and beautiful formal gardens, this was the country seat of the Legh family for over 600 years until it was donated to the National Trust in 1946 by Richard Legh, 3rd Lord Newton. The imposing Hall is an interesting blend of Georgian, Elizabethan and Regency architecture and contains a wealth of fine period furniture, paintings and tapestries as well as a splendid collection of English clocks. Outside you can stroll through the exquisite Victorian Gardens which include an Orangery by Wyatt. With free roaming herds of Red Deer, the unusual landmark known as The Cage and its own Countryside Centre, a trip to Lyme Park will provide you with a day out to remember.

Lyme Park, Disley, Stockport Tel: 0663 762023

Not far from here, enjoying a peaceful rural setting in the small village of **Kettleshulme**, **The Swan** is a delightful country pub

272

Gawsworth Old Rectory, Nr Macclesfield

dating back to the 15th century. John and Angela Adamson are the friendly proprietors who offer a warm welcome to visitors and locals alike. The Swan is everything you expect of a traditional village pub, attractively decorated throughout, with a cosy bar serving Marstons Real Ales. Homemade bar snacks are available at lunchtime only. Open evenings only during the week and both lunchtime and evenings at the weekend, this is the perfect place to call in after a day exploring this lovely corner of Cheshire.

The Swan, Macclesfield Road, Kettleshulme Tel: 0663 732943

And so we reach the end of our tour of Lancashire, Cheshire and the Isle of Man, having uncovered just some of the hidden treasures of the region. No doubt you will discover a few of your own, but we feel sure that any places you visit would be pleased to know that you heard about them through Hidden Places.

Tourist Information Centres

ACCRINGTON Gothic House, St James Street Tel: 0254 386807

ALTRINCHAM Stamford New Road Tel: 061 941 7337

BIRKENHEAD Woodside Ferry Terminal Tel: 051 647 6780

BLACKBURN King George's Hall, Northgate Tel: 0254 53277

BLACKPOOL 1 Clifton Street Tel: 0253 21623/25212

BLACKPOOL 87a Coronation Street Tel: 0253 23041

BLACKPOOL Pleasure Beach, 525 Ocean Boulevard Tel: 0253 403223

BOLTON Town Hall, Victoria Square Tel: 0204 364333

BURNLEY Burnley Mechanics, Manchester Road Tel: 0282 455485

BURY Derby Hall, Market Street Tel: 061 705 5111

CHARNOCK RICHARD M6 Service Area (Northbound) Tel: 0257 793773

CHESTER Town Hall, Northgate Street Tel: 0244 317962

CHESTER Visitor Centre, Vicars Lane Tel: 0244 351609/318916

CONGLETON Town Hall, High Street Tel: 0260 271095

FLEETWOOD Ferry Dock, The Esplanade Tel: 0253 773953

FORTON, M6 Services, Bay Horse, Lancaster Tel: 0524 792181

GARSTANG, Discovery Centre, Council Offices, High Street Tel: 0995 602125

KNUTSFORD Council Offices, Toft Road Tel: 0565 632611/632210

LANCASTER 29 Castle Hill Tel: 0524 847472

LIVERPOOL Merseyside Welcome Centre, Clayton Square Tel: 051 709 3631

LYTHAM ST. ANNES The Square Tel: 0253 725610

MACCLESFIELD Council Offices, Town Hall Tel: 0625 504114

MANCHESTER Town Hall Extension, Lloyd Street Tel: 061 236 9900

MANCHESTER AIRPORT International Arrivals Area, T1 & T2 Tel: 061 436 3344

NANTWICH Beam Street Tel: 0270 623914

NEW BRIGHTON Floral Pavilion, Virginia Road Tel: 051 638 7144

OLDHAM 84 Union Street Tel: 061 678 4654

PRESTON The Guildhall, Lancaster Road Tel: 0772 53731

RAWTENSTALL 41/45 Key Street, Rossendale Tel: 0706 226590

ROCHDALE The Clock Tower, Town Hall Tel: 0706 356592

RUNCORN 57/61 Church Street Tel: 0928 576776

SADDLEWORTH High Street, Uppermill, Oldham Tel: 045787 4093/0336

SANDBACH Motorway Service Area, M6 Northbound Tel: 0270 760460

SOUTHPORT 112 Lord Street Tel: 0704 533333

STOCKPORT Graylaw House, Chestergate Tel: 061 474 3320/ 474 3321

TODMORDEN 15 Burnley Road Tel: 0706 818181

WARRINGTON 21 Rylands Road Tel: 0925 36501/444400

WIDNES Municipal Building, Kingsway Tel: 051 424 2061

WIGAN Trencherfield Mill, Wigan Pier Tel: 0942 825677

ISLE OF MAN

BALLASALLA Airport Information Desk, Ronaldsway Airport Tel: 0624 823311

CASTLETOWN The Old Grammar School, The Car Park

DOUGLAS Harris Promenade Tel: 0624 686766

LAXEY Old Fire House, nr. Laxey Wheel Tel: 0624 862007

ONCHAN Village Commisioners Public Library, 10 Elm Tree Road Tel: 0624 621228

PEEL Town Hall, Derby Road Tel: 0624 842341

PORT ERIN Commissioners Office, Station Road Tel: 0624 832298

PORT ST. MARY Commissioners Office, Town Hall Tel: 0624 832101

RAMSEY The Library, Town Hall Tel: 0624 812228

Index

H

I

K

L

M

N

O

P

R

S

Salford 15
Sandbach 212
Sawley 55
Scarisbrick 156
Silverdale 89
Slaidburn 65
Southport 156
St. Helens 165
Stockport 22
Stretton 235
Styal 262
Sunderland Point 83

T

Tarporley 230
Tattenhall 236
Thurnham 86
Thurstaton 172
Tilston 234
Tosside 66
Trawden Forest 34

U

Uppermill 21

W

Waddington 61
Warmingham 210
Warrington 178
Weaverham 194
Weavers' Cottage 42
West Bradford 61
West Kirby 172
Weston 218
Wettenhall 207
Whalley 44
Wharton 209
White Hough 33
Whitegate 206
Whittington 75
Widnes 178

Wigan 17
Willaston 174
Wilmslow 260
Winsford 209
Worsley 16
Wycoller 34

THE HIDDEN PLACES

If you would like to have any of the titles currently available in this series, please complete this coupon and send to:

M & M Publishing Ltd
Tryfan House, Warwick Drive,
Hale, Altrincham, Cheshire, WA15 9EA

	Each	Qty
Scotland	£ 5.90	......
Northumberland & Durham	£ 5.90	......
The Lake District & Cumbria	£ 5.90	......
Yorkshire and Humberside	£ 5.90	......
Lancashire & Cheshire	£ 5.90	......
North Wales	£ 5.90	......
South Wales	£ 5.90	......
The Welsh Borders	£ 5.90	......
The Cotswolds (Gloucestershire & Wiltshire)	£ 5.90	......
Thames and Chilterns	£ 5.90	......
East Anglia (Norfolk & Suffolk)	£ 5.90	......
The South East (Surrey, Sussex and Kent)	£ 5.90	......
Dorest, Hampshire and the Isle of Wight	£ 5.90	......
Somerset, Avon and Dorset	£ 5.90	......
Heart of England	£ 5.90	......
Devon and Cornwall	£ 5.90	......
Set of any Five	£20.00	
Total	£	

Price includes Postage and Packing

NAME...

ADDRESS...

....

...............................POST CODE...................................

Please make cheques payable to: M & M Publishing Ltd

NOTES